Understanding Everyday Experience
Series Editor: Laurie Taylor

IRMA KURTZ

Loneliness

Basil Blackwell · Oxford

First published 1983
Basil Blackwell Publisher Limited
108 Cowley Road, Oxford OX4 1JF, England

British Library Cataloguing in Publication Data

Kurtz, Irma
    Loneliness.—(Understanding everyday experience)
    1. Loneliness
    I. Title
    302.5'45   BF575.L7

    ISBN 0—631—12578—7
    ISBN 0—631—13084—5 Pbk

Typesetting by System 4 Associates, Gerrards Cross
Printed in Great Britain by The Camelot Press

Contents

Preface

'Hello. You busy? Sorry to ring so late but I was just wondering if you got my postcard. You did? Oh, good. Only the thing was that I didn't actually have your address with me and had to have a guess at the number of the house. 164. Is that right? Oh good. So you got it? How are you keeping?'

I suppose that the people who get that sort of pointless late night call from me know that I must be feeling pretty lonely if I've had to grub around for such an unlikely excuse before dialling their number. But then they too, at some time or another, have probably made just such calls.

We don't admit easily to loneliness, it sounds so much like a personal failing, an admission that we haven't been trying hard enough, that we've become too self-centred. There is even a stock response to any such confession which catches that element of hostility. 'Lonely? Really? Well, why don't you do what they say in the agony columns and go out and join a few clubs?'

That's not the sort of 'snap out of it' advice you'd find in Irma Kurtz's regular column in *Cosmopolitan*. Her great strength as an 'agony aunt' has always been her readiness to resist pat solutions, to use the complexities of her own experience as a starting point and guide to the likely subtleties of her correspondent's distress. And, as she observes in the following pages, that distress, however much it may be clothed in the language of orthodox questions — 'Shall I have his child?'; 'Does she love me?'; Shall we live together?'; 'What can I say to my mother?' — is so often about the fear, or the actual experience, of loneliness.

Irma Kurtz would probably not like to hear her column described as a problem page, for much of her advice seeks to assure those who report 'problems' that their concerns or anxieties are shared with their neighbours. They are not so much problems, specialized matters for the therapist or the analyst, as the dilemmas and difficulties of everyday life.

It is this recognition, more than any other quality, which gives her present book on loneliness such a universal appeal, and which makes it such a welcome and suitable addition to this series of volumes.

Laurie Taylor

Introduction

Loneliness: the lighthouse keeper knows as much about loneliness as the psychologist. Maybe you know more than either of them. Although we can discuss what constitutes the feeling of loneliness and what social factors exacerbate it, we cannot know how that feeling — or any feeling — feels for another. This very inaccessibility of others' feelings, the feelings even of those we love, is a strand of loneliness.

Because I am an agony aunt on a glossy magazine, I am forced to be aware all the time of how much loneliness there is in our world, and so I am undertaking this book to organize what I have observed and to try to bring greater understanding to my own condition and to the letters I receive from others.

Don't you find,' asked a friend of mine, a psychiatrist it so happens, 'that the trouble is always loneliness?' Is he right? Is loneliness always the problem? If so, then the woman who writes to me out of the dizziness of promiscuity, and the distraught mother of five children, and the middle-aged man creating himself an ulcer are as lonely as the shy, overweight, 17-year-old virgin. And if that is so, if loneliness is the mainstem from which other distresses arise, then I am about to embark on the daunting investigation of absolutely everything about absolutely all of us! The swaggering bravado of such a venture could discourage an academic and would appal a scientist, but a journalist and busybody like me finds it irresistible.

In any case, it is probably as much of a distraction from anxiety to read as it is to write (at least, both activities can make a change from more usual anxieties), so I hope at least the length of the reading will ease your loneliness as the length of the writing did mine.

1

Utopians in Exile

> It is not syphilis which is the occupational disease of the prostitute, but loneliness.
>
> Polly Adler, *A House is not a Home*

Do you imagine primitive man was lonely? Was he lonelier huddled with his tribe than the Prime Minister is at Number Ten? Is it really lonelier at the top than at the bottom of a mineshaft, say, or in a submarine? Is loneliness an occupational hazard only for prostitutes, or does it afflict housewives? Is the prison warder as lonely as the prisoner, or is he perhaps much lonelier? Is the gifted child less lonely than the handicapped child, or is neither as lonely as the average child? Is a married man less lonely than a rake? Is a woman who writes in to an advice column as lonely as another who writes to nobody? Are you lonelier than I, and are we both lonelier than an Australian Aborigine on his solitary walkabout?

There is not one of us who hasn't been aware at some point, or always, that he is or could be lonely. Few of us have not known the impression, sudden as a *déja vu*, that we were not born into this culture but were exiled to it from a better place. Some of us feel a surge of panic as soon as we find ourselves

3

alone with nobody else there to define us to ourselves, to tell us who we are, to assure us *that* we are. And most of us have known the sorrow of discovering that what appeared to be a mating, a twinning almost, was deception and no real escape from aloneness. It makes us no less lonely to know that we all live with loneliness, flee it, return to it, cry about it, sing about it, yet are for the most part uncertain about its nature. Because loneliness is within us and outside us, because each of us contains his own loneliness and also increases the loneliness of others, because there are characteristics of our society which exacerbate loneliness, and because we cannot hold loneliness or see it but only feel it, loneliness has become the carthorse for our misery, dragging behind it weights as disparate as stymied lust and the despair of genius. Just as cancer serves contemporary death, so loneliness serves contemporary unhappiness and neurosis.

Is it any wonder that we have trouble defining loneliness or that we cannot always distinguish it from other feelings? For example, both adolescents and their elders, who are supposed to know better but do not always feel better, frequently complain of their loneliness, although they are in the midst of society, and what they really mean is they want sex. Sexual frustration may be irritation or misery, but ought we to call it loneliness? I do not think so. Some psychiatrists maintain that loneliness results from the severing of the umbilical cord. This piece of common sense makes loneliness sound downright wholesome without in the least explaining it. Then there are market researchers to tell potential advertisers that poor people are lonelier than the prosperous, the old feel lonelier than the young and housewives feel

4

3 per cent lonelier than working spinsters. All this may be helpful for the marketing of soap or soup, but we still are left knowing for sure only that loneliness is a feeling and, like all other feelings, must be subjective and therefore impossible to measure, to weigh or to compare. Loneliness is susceptible only to description. Ironically, in those moments when a man is busy trying to describe his loneliness to an interviewer, he is relatively free from loneliness and is therefore describing that strange, amorphous, indescribable thing called a memory of that strange, amorphous and indescribable feeling called loneliness.

Not knowing for sure what loneliness is or where it comes from, mind you, doesn't stop us trying to 'cure' it, or trying to lay blame for it (generally upon the society that suffers from it). Nor has our ignorance about the nature of loneliness prevented the well-meaning as well as messianic upstarts, charlatans and political zealots from making capital out of it. What bad men understand even better than many good men is that loneliness is in some way connected to a passionate, frustrated longing in all of us to be worthy, to be caring, to serve, to be brothers, and to help build Utopia. Shiva Naipaul describes how this longing for a community of good men can draw naive people into the circle of what may be called true evil, that is, the horror, degradation and ultimate self-destruction of the megalomaniac Jim Jones's 'People's Temple':

In Jim Jones and the People's Temple they felt they had at last found what...they had always been searching for. The Temple preached a political and social philosophy they could understand. It talked about service to those less fortunate than

5

oneself....It talked about equality. It talked about universal brotherhood....what really drew them was the atmosphere of caring, the sense of community, the feeling that one belonged to a large, multi-racial family....[1]

Although we all may long to belong to a cherishing and generous society, it does take simplicity of mind to think we will achieve it easily, or even at all; and a lot of people consider it more sophisticated to imagine they can end their loneliness by perfecting themselves, and never mind anyone else. For instance, a lot of lonely Americans who would not dream of following a Jim Jones to Guyana prefer to seek happiness in therapeutic groups like those of Fritz Perls, the originator of Gestalt Therapy, at Essalen in Big Sur, where they raise their voices in a hymn marked by its petulance, yet nevertheless hopeful of some kind of brotherhood.

I do my thing and you do your thing.
I am not in this world to live up to your expecations,
And you are not in this world to live up to mine.
You are you, and I am I,
And if by chance we find each other, it's beautiful.
If not, it can't be helped.[2]

Personally, were I given a choice between the soft drink of Guyana, the bitter distillation of Perls and even the saccharin of someone like Billy Graham, I think I'd prefer to drink deeper of my own loneliness. Nevertheless, who would say the quest to end loneliness in our society is 'wrong' simply because it has often gone wrong? And who would say it's hopeless simply because no one can see it anywhere being accomplished? All I myself feel brave enough to say about loneliness is just this: shame, solitude and romantic delusions are components of our loneliness, but its key is loss — loss of nature, loss of God, loss of each other. And the apogee of loneliness is loss of self.

2

All the Lonely People

All the lonely people, where do they all come
  from?
                    Lennon/McCartney, 'Eleanor Rigby'

Have we always felt loneliness? Why should we
suppose human emotions remain static and immut-
able throughout time, while all else changes? The
words 'loneliness', 'alone' and 'lonesome' have been
with us for quite a while, but only relatively recently
have they taken on the colour of deep dejection. To
be alone has not always been a bad thing. Although
God Himself is said in the Bible to have decided, 'it
is not good that man should be alone,' doesn't it
seem that He was being not sentimental but rather
pragmatic about his experiment, Adam, who was not
so perfectly in God's image that he could produce
generations without mate, and who was lacking in
divine symmetry? After all, if a mere companion were
all Adam needed, then why not use the rib to make
another man? That wouldn't have been such a bad
idea. But it was a woman who was needed, Adam's
complement and troublemaker; and we are told that
in due course out of their precarious togetherness
came loneliness into the world. Another ancient myth

says despairs and griefs were waiting inside a box opened by the willful girl, Pandora. And yet another fairytale tells us our sorrows were the creation of Psyche, disobedient mortal bride, who lit the lamp and looked at her divine husband, and whose punishment for this infraction of house rules was the existential pains visited upon us all. The reason loneliness (and other ills) arrived in a previously untroubled world, according to all these major myths was a woman, who is usually referred to as sly, deceitful or just gullible. (I myself would call her nothing more sinister than curious.)

Thus the message of these texts and allegories seems to be that when we cease to be contented with the *status quo*, when we question, dare, defy and try to bend our environment to our needs — when, in other words, we act with human brilliance and precociousness — loneliness and other agonies attack us. Loneliness is part of the price we pay for knowledge. Separateness from holy dicta, from nature and, in due course, from each other and each from himself was the dark cloud that followed us out of blissful ignorance, and shame was our burden. The road from Eden led more or less directly to narcissism, pornography, addiction, the divorce courts and other symptoms of loneliness in our time.

Few of us, and certainly not a non-believer like me, think of Eden as a real garden with trees, and rivers, and cuddly tigers rolling in the grass; and those fundamentalists who do imagine Eden this way are looking backwards — never a very profitable way to look — for a solution to their loneliness. Eden represents for me a state of balance and perfection, an ideal never to exist or as likely to exist in the dim future as it did in the cloudy past. Whether the gates of that great state

9

once swung closed behind us or are swinging slowly open to let us in does not really matter, for the point that concerns us now is only that we are in motion and our condition is changing. We make gains, and for each of them we suffer losses. We move away from faith towards Mars; we analyse the functions of our bodies more, but comprehend the purpose of our minds less; we are gratified by flashes of scientific understanding but, to judge from our divorce rate, disappointed in our understanding of each other. The confusion that results from these discrepancies is called alienation, and its chief manifestation has become loneliness.

It was the poets, notably the English Romantics, who made of loneliness a personal and sad experience (in fact, a lonely experience), resembling post-coital *tristesse* more than the passion of, say, St Augustine. Keats, for example, wrote to his muse in 'Hyperion':

A solitary sorrow best befits
Thy lips, and antheming a lonely grief....

Coleridge wrote in 'The Rime of the Ancient Mariner':

O Wedding-Guest! This soul hath been
Alone on a wide, wide sea:
'So lonely 'twas, that God himself
Scarce seemed there to be....

As for Lord Byron, he celebrated the plaintive loneliness of after-love with a melancholy enthusiasm not to be equalled until those American torch-songs decades later which were hardly ever about anything but the feeling of loneliness. As Elvis once sang:

Now, since my baby left me
I've found a new place to dwell.
It's down at the bottom of Lonely Street,
It's called Heartbreak Hotel....
I get so lonely I could die....

Much more recently, like a lot of what formerly
was fodder for poets — like sex, love and war —
loneliness was claimed as a social condition, a suitable
study for sociologists, psychotherapists, advice
columnists, even politicians. In November 1981, for
example, a minority party candidate in a crucial
by-election declared loneliness his main issue and
advocated the establishment of a 'national lonely
line' as the main plank in his platform, more than
a century too late, fortunately, to solace John Keats'
muse. One American transactional analyst, Ira A.
Tanner, pronounced the new status of loneliness a
disease outright in the introduction to his book
Loneliness: the Fear of Love: 'with the disease of
loneliness we have not always known where to hit....
Today huge throngs of people are suffering from the
disease and going untreated because they are not
aware of the nature of their ailment....'[1] How dis-
concerting to learn that those who suffer from a
disease need to know its nature in order to be treated
for it! I'd always thought it was enough to find a
doctor who knew the nature of the disease. But could
it be that the nature of loneliness is unknown to even
the loneliest doctor?

'People need People' is the chapter of Dr Tony
Lake's book *Loneliness* in which he writes, 'loneliness
is a behavioural illness....Lonely people cannot share
because they have nobody to share with....'[2]
Having nobody to share with is a pretty good

11

reason for not sharing, just as having no food is an excusable way to starve to death. But if sharing could really end loneliness, then we would have no lonely mothers, and no lonely fathers, and no lonely flat-mates, and no lonely Communists. The general trap, I think, among those who write about loneliness is to treat loneliness as a nasty new pathology for which we must discover a 'cure'. (In Dr Lake's opinion, by the way, treatment involves mastering eye contact, and in Dr Tanner's more sophisticated opinion, the remedy is to cease to be 'afraid to love'.)

In my own opinion, loneliness is not a sickness, nor is it, in a social sense, what Mother Teresa of Calcutta is alleged to have called 'the world's most serious problem'. This quotation was ascribed to her by a man who is writing a book on 'how loneliness may be cured' and who published a letter in London's *New Standard* asking for suggestions or anecdotes from 'those who have conquered loneliness in themselves or in others'. Loneliness is a common experience, and the consensus is that it results in a bad feeling. Since it is generally held that bad feelings ought not to be tolerated by a good society, books and even whole careers (that of an agony aunt, for example) are based upon eliminating loneliness from the populace. But are bad feelings necessarily diseases? The bad feeling of grief, for instance — isn't it natural and necessary? And can't the bad feeling of anger be useful, creative and crusading? Feeling bad is feeling too, and surely the only way to stop having bad feelings would be to stop feeling anything at all. And the only way to stop risking bad thought would be to stop thinking. And the only way to eschew all bad experiences would be to do nothing at all.

Catatonia is too high a price to pay for 'curing' the bad feeling of loneliness. If loneliness is, as I think it is, part of the ineluctable price our society pays for progress, and if it is the price an individual must pay for privacy and free thought, then are we not better advised to learn how to tolerate it rather than how to 'cure' it? From where I sit, behind the desk of a glossy women's magazine, it seems to me that most pain results from our desperate, ill-chosen attempts to 'cure' loneliness — from versions of Jim Jones's People's Temple, for example, from fashionable therapies, from dreams of eternal romantic couplings, from excesses of flesh and from what I can only call a spiritual laziness that expects a personal miracle at no expense of energy or self. Loneliness is the space within where once there was something or maybe someday there will be something. Nobody can 'cure' a space; all we can do is try to begin to fill it with something sustaining.

3

Childhood: a New Estate

'The crow must have flown away, I think,' said Alice: 'I'm so glad it's gone. I thought it was the night coming on.'

I wish *I* could manage to be glad! the Queen said. 'Only I never can remember the rule. You must be very happy, living in this wood, and being glad whenever you like!'

Only it is so *very* lonely here!' Alice said in a melancholy voice; and at the thought of her loneliness two large tears came rolling down her cheeks.

'Oh, don't go on like that!' cried the poor Queen, wringing her hands in despair. 'Consider what a great girl you are....Consider anything, only don't cry!'

Alice could not help laughing at this, even in the midst of her tears. 'Can *you* keep from crying by considering things?' she asked.

'That's the way it's done,' the Queen said with great decision: 'Nobody can do two things at once, you know....'

Lewis Carroll, *Through the Looking-Glass*

One of the rare experiences absolutely everyone in

our society has in common is having been a child, and another one is loneliness. If these two conditions are universal, then doesn't it seem that they must share some interesting connections? Not all societies have childhood, and not all societies have loneliness. Maybe there was a time when our society had neither. In more than one sense, the youngest class among us is the class of children.

Ivan Illich has written:

> Childhood, as distinct from infancy, adolescence, or youth was unknown to most historical periods. Some Christian centuries did not even have an eye for its bodily proportions. Artists depicted the infant as a miniature adult....Before our century ....childhood belonged to the bourgeoisie. The worker's child, the peasant's child, and the nobleman's child all dressed the way their fathers dressed, played the way their fathers played, and were hanged by the neck as were their fathers. After the discovery of 'childhood' by the bourgeoisie all this changed. Only some Churches continued to respect for some time the dignity and maturity of the young.[1]

Respect for the 'dignity and maturity' of children on the part of the Churches simply meant that it was commonly held that after the age of seven children could suffer in Hell for their sins. Nowadays we frequently make them suffer on earth for ours. Whether children are a 'discovered' class, an invented one or a class emancipated by the machines that replaced them as field hands, apprenticed artisans, home-helps, miners and urban labour staff is arguable, but certainly with the creation of the class of children among all social classes there came a radical change in the role of parents. No longer were parents there simply to procreate, nourish their offspring for a a necessary period, then ship them out, like a perfectly formed pygmy tribe, into the adult world. For all the difficulties of life in those dark ages before the invention of childhood, how much easier the parental role must have been. To be a parent without children! It is as enticing as, say, the thought of Paris without Parisians! How natural and undemanding to produce babies as other creatures in nature do and soon set their toddling feet *en route*, sons in their fathers' footsteps and daughters in the footsteps of Eve. If once upon a time there were no delinquent children, neurotic children, problem children, neglected children, battered children, that was quite simply because there were no children. Theoretical education for the mass of young people was rudimentary; classical education hardly existed at all except for a smattering of Scripture; and only a thoroughly practical education was vital. In other words, until this century education for most young people was pretty much what some politicians and educationists want us to revert to now. Even the young noblemen learned skills and graces essential to their future as heirs of their fathers. Nobody needed to know much more than his parents had known, and I dare say it could be successfully argued that those who chose to know more were lonely people.

Each time a new class is formed in our society and hedged around from the rest of us, a new source of isolation is created, particularly when that class, like the class of children, is patently dependent upon a ruling class and isolated from it by numerous rules generally enforced by punishments. Children, for example, have bedtimes, and these are arranged to precede the hours in which grown-ups have fun, have fights, have drink, have each other, have parties, have too much and generally let their hair down. Like the members of every ruling class, adults know it is dangerous for them to be seen at play by their underlings, as it might 'put ideas into their heads'. The first thing we expect from the class of children is obedience, and so very obedient do we expect them to be, it could seem to a visitor from some earlier century that we invented children out of a need to make something pay attention to us and obey our most whimsical and illogical demands. Mind you, if he were an experienced and observant time traveller, he could warn us that whenever we create a subservient class we also create a class of potential rebels. The fate of rebellious children, of course, is that they are destined to grow up. This is a tragedy they share with other revolutionaries.

When the prehistoric toddler wandered out he learned fast to distinguish what was good from what was deadly or he perished. Our children are expected to learn an infinitely more complex set of rules and systems, and they'd better learn their lessons well or they fail. There is nothing that produces isolation and the bad feeling of loneliness in a child as effectively as failure, especially when it threatens to cut off the approval and, it could seem, the love of those whose love and approval is central to any child's sense of his own worth and even of his own existence: his big bosses, his parents.

In Japan, where education is highly competitive and early failure means permanent social disaster, every examination season is marked by a wave of adolescent suicides. In our society, maybe because we don't have the tradition of literal self-sacrifice, suicides do take place among the young, but they are less numerous and generally precipitated by something personal and special to the individual. (At my own school there were two suicides one year and both at exam time. Both girls were the children of celebrated intellectuals, and one was the daughter of the President of the first black college in the United States.) For whatever reason a suicide is undertaken — as revenge or punishment, merely as an attempt, out of fear, out of genuine despair — it is the loneliest of acts, for, unlike natural death, it must take place in isolation, and it claims the total responsibility of the deathbound person: the suicide does, is done to, and is undone by, his own hand. Such singleness of mind is so terrifyingly lonely that we are quick to decide that the person who assumes such responsibility for himself is actually behaving 'irresponsibly' and is not in his right mind. The thought of children driven out of their minds is a hideous one, but even more numerous than physical suicides among us are the children defeated in spirit, who retreat into lethargy or other antisocial behaviour which is a kind of suicide. We generally educate our children not to make them brilliant at something but to make them fair at virtually everything; and therefore it is not only the failed child who is in the isolation that produces the bad feelings of estrangement and loneliness but also the child who is too clever for his own good. The halls of our schools all contain children in whom the seeds of loneliness that exist in every human being are beginning to swell and to sprout.

Because of the complexity of the material children

must master — or at least memorize — they can no longer be taught by their parents but only by 'experts', another class only as old as childhood and dependent upon the creation of children: the schoolroom teachers. As any parent of a school-age child knows, these teachers are often heard to complain that teaching is being left to their expertise and that parents have a duty to involve themselves in the work of the classroom. (Mind you, children are being taught in America increasingly by computers, television sets, and 'educational games'; none of these has ever yet been heard to complain about anything, but they surely cannot much help a child predisposed to loneliness.) What classroom teachers don't always understand is that no matter how many parent—teacher meetings are dutifully attended, no matter how parents vote in national elections and no matter how many rock cakes are baked for school fêtes, the fact is that children are being increasingly educated in ways and subjects their parents never learned themselves and do not know.

Education equips children for everyday life in a world that we grown-ups no longer comprehend on a technological, intellectual or moral level. I'm no chicken, I'll grant you, but it is not a century ago that I was a child in New York City. On a recent visit there, my host's son — a 12-year-old — instructed me to walk always on the outside of the pavement because muggers like dark doorways, never to remain in a subway car with only two or three other passengers and always to carry a dollar bill wrapped around some cut up newspaper, presumably so that when given the choice between my money and my life, I wouldn't be placed in existential dilemma. The difference between his street savvy and mine (don't step on the cracks of the pavement or a goblin will get you!) represents centuries, not mere decades.

Not just current knowledge but even history has changed radically. The average schoolchild now can probably name most astronauts since the first one, and he knows what the moon is made of. But when asked a few years ago 'Who was Hitler?' none of a class of thirty 12-year-old Londoners could answer correctly; even those who had the right idea couldn't spell it; and one little boy said he was 'king of the Jews'. Whether or not world-shaking events happen faster now, they are reported virtually instantaneously, and a moment after it has happened, history becomes 'ancient'. One of the arguments put forward for breakfast television in Britain was that we need to know what has happened in the world while we have been asleep. I wonder why we 'need' or even want to know? Presumably, so we can forget it faster. The giddy speed of happenings and shortness of memory contribute to gaps of understanding between the generations. Nowhere is that gap wider than in moral issues, and a family that does not accept tradition or the Church as adjudicator in these questions can reveal a difference much, much more serious than years.

In short, although we keep our children at home longer now than ever before, in may ways we have increasingly less to share with them than might be expected, and much less to share with them than in the days when they were small, working adults. Sometimes it seems to me that having created children and provided them with their own areas of amusement and education, we have lost them. People are easily isolated from each other by differences in their knowledge. Isn't that one chief argument in favour of doing away with private education? At a typical American university like the one I attended, members of the English faculty might never meet a botanist and care very little to meet one. Ideally, I suppose, education should be affectionate instruction between generations; however, children now need different skills, often taught in a different language and in a different way from the way their parents learned. The only means of narrowing the gap between generations and bringing children out of alienation from the grown-up world would be to let grown-ups learn with their children — in fact, to open education now relegated to the class of children to everyone — but that is an attractive ideal which has functioned in a few small communities and is not feasible on a large scale. Partly it is not practicable because not many adults are willing to admit to less than perfect wisdom before their children.

What isolates children most of all from adults and ripens the harvest of loneliness is not just that we expect them to know as much as their classmates and to do as well; it is also that there are things we do not expect them to know or to do. Carl Jung wrote:

It would never have occurred to me to speak of my experiences openly, nor of my dream of the phallus in the underground temple....As a matter of fact, I did not say anything about the phallus dream until I was sixty-five. I may have spoken about the other experiences to my wife, but only in later years. A strict taboo hung over all these matters, inherited from my childhood. I could never have talked about them with friends.
My entire youth can be understood in terms

21

of this secret. It induced in me an almost unendurable loneliness....[2]

We are still reluctant to allow our children their secrets and we suspect that all their secrets are salacious or seditious. Thus we force our children to make secrets of thoughts, dreams, experiences and impressions they might share with us, to the advantage of their future well-being and understanding, if they did not fear our scorn and disapproval.

> The consequence of my...involvement with things which neither I nor anyone else could understand, was an extreme loneliness. I was going about laden with thoughts of which I could speak to no one: they would only have been misunderstood. I felt the gulf between the external world and the interior world of images in its most painful form. I could not yet see that interaction of both worlds which I now understand. I saw only an irreconcilable contradiction between 'inner' and 'outer'.... Later...I did all in my power to convey to my intimates a new way of seeing things. I knew that if I did not succeed, I would be condemned to absolute isolation.[3]

Loneliness may be the price of enlightenment, but to keep secrets while living as an innocent in the household is too much for a child to bear without being forced too soon into alienation and eventually into the misty no-man's-land between the 'inner' and 'outer' worlds, into that alienation from self which is the anguish we call loneliness. There are children who are afraid to tell their parents they have taken drugs or even that they have become addicts.

(Do they have reason to be afraid? We read regularly about parents who can think of nothing more helpful to do with addicted offspring than turn them over to the police — just as I still receive letters from pregnant teenagers put out of their homes by mothers and fathers who love the good opinion of others more than they love.) There are children terrified in secret of their homosexual longings. There are girls who will not go to the family doctor for a pregnancy test or contraceptives because they are afraid the doctor will report them to their parents. A lot of these young people write to agony aunts, but in a world of more generous spirit the agony aunts would be replaced by parents. There are 10-year-olds afraid of a certain teacher, or a street, or another child, but much more afraid to discuss their fears with adults who are contemptuous of children's terror. And there are lots of children who have sacrificed their expression of dreams, ambitions and fantasies to parental scorn, thus condemning themselves to 'absolute isolation'.

The rights and privileges of a ruling class impose upon that class responsibility for the class that is ruled. If we must rule our children, then it is our responsibility to educate them — or, rather, to see to it they are educated by others — and we are also expected to give them a moral code of behaviour, albeit one we do not follow ourselves. But the most important of our responsibilities is a very new one, even towards the relatively new class of children: we are supposed to make them happy. To this end — the happiness of our children — we seem willing to make every sacrifice of honesty. Just as slave owners in the South of America imagined they were good to 'their people' because 'their people' sang so sweetly around the campfires, so we parents look for evidence that we have successfully created an idyllic world of childhood for our offspring and an environment free from all the ugliness existing in our adult world. 'They'll see wickedness soon enough,' we say, as if our children were blind as kittens and could not already see the iniquities of the world around them. As if nightmares were not more often the result of unwelcome truths suppressed than of some celluloid-and-ketchup make-believe. As if, for that matter, in their own school yard there was no aggression, bigotry, depravity and criminality. We adults want to hear our children's laughter, their songs and their prayers to a God whom we ourselves no longer hold in awe. In America, where happiness is considered a goal more specific than simple relief from misery, which is how the British tend to see it, whole communities of parents attend lectures on 'Parental Effectiveness' where they are instructed never to scold, never to say 'no', always to engage their offspring in dialogue and thus, at any expense of their own sanity and honesty, to keep the kiddies happy. I once listened to a harassed American mother submit her 4-year-old to this Socratic technique to make him agree that it was 'bad for him' to eat an iced lolly before lunch. The child listened to his mother with resignation while he was in the very process of devouring her thesis. It was a real demonstration of confusion, condescension and alienation.

Having invented childhood, we try to create a charming, safe place where it can be lived among us but apart from us; and if our children are learning how to be deeply, painfully lonely in their isolation from us, if they are learning not to communicate what they are honestly thinking, if the gap between what they know and what we permit them to tell us they know increases to the point where 'inner' and 'outer' may never be reconciled, we do not always seem to notice; and this is an oversight which to a child, quite justifiably, means we do not care.

4

Heirs to Loneliness

> Reflected in the still pool he saw many white shapes with long necks and golden bills, and, without thinking, he looked for [his] dull grey body....Instead, he beheld beneath him a beautiful white swan!...the duckling thought that it was worth while having undergone all the persecution and loneliness that he had passed through, as otherwise he would never have known what it was to be really happy.
>
> Hans Christian Andersen, 'The Ugly Duckling'

A six-year-old beggar in Calcutta or a 12-year-old prostitute in Bangkok would be confounded by a description of adventure playgrounds where adults are forbidden entrance, or strip clubs and brothels where children are not allowed. But in the Western world we need our children, and the invention of childhood is vital to our way of life. It would be a wise courtesy to the child and to the adult he is becoming to put a swing door on the nursery that will allow the inmate out before he is driven to distraction in his isolation from a world he was born to inherit. We are always pleased to notice the child who lives within every grown-up — women are particularly pleased to see the child within every man — but we find it much more difficult to acknowledge that within each child an adult is waiting. That waiting adult needs to learn a trade and to acquire the skills of survival in our community, but he already possesses personality and dignity which, if they are slighted, mocked or neglected, can fragment and shatter into the confusion that makes loneliness so painful. When evident truths are denied by adults (those truths a child sees clearly for himself: truths about power and responsibility, about angels and devils, about sex and mercy) and when talents are scorned or rejected (talents like the one most children have for connecting disparate concepts, for solitude, and even for making trouble), then that loss of self which is the dark core of loneliness can start to take place.

Children like structure, and they must be shown our rules, but they are also in every sense what A. S. Neill, in his book *Summerhill*,[1] calls our 'fellow citizens'. They ought to be let into our mysteries as soon as they show themselves ready; and we must confess to them our own confusion, as we would to good friends; and they must be respected, not judged. It is certainly not my opinion alone that the abiding terrors of adulthood are often lodged in childhood. Great schools of psychoanalysis are built on that very cornerstone. Of the adult terrors, loneliness is ubiquitous, and that is why in this discussion about loneliness I am bound to make such a fuss about childhood.

As we are living in a world where privacy is a requirement and solitude a strong possibility at some point in every life, our children will be better equipped for their inheritance and better able to avoid the fear and shame attached to solitude if they are granted privacy virtually from the beginning of their consciousness, and if they are encouraged to survive fearlessly in solitude. For instance, the adult inside every child is entitled to private correspondence and to friends of his own choosing; this should go without needing to be said, but anyone who counsels young people knows that it does not. That adult is also entitled to have his opinions heard in their turn and his confidences taken seriously, for they are serious. He is entitled to be given truthful answers to any questions he asks, for it is his questions that tell us what he is prepared to know. He is entitled to tell even an unpalatable truth and to be heard without rejection of that truth, which is a rejection of him. And he should be encouraged to tell all his truths because lies are painfully lonely.

We must all be allowed our own secrets and no fellow citizen in a free society should be forced to make a secret of the truth, for therein lies the essence of shame, first cousin to loneliness which is, as much as it is anything else and more than it is most things, the failure to enjoy our own company. A daughter need not tell her mother when she has her first lover — why should she? But she ought not to be afraid to tell her mother if she needs to, or afraid to buy a contraceptive in case her mother should find it. Mind you, the child of any parent who goes through her pockets or her handbag is already predisposed to shame, isolation and loneliness. Dark secrets are furtive and lonely, yes, but they can exist only when people refuse to accept dark truths.

'Rebecca is a bright little girl, but she spends too much time on her own....' This is a teacher's comment, and not an uncommon one, on the report of an 8-year-old girl. Naturally, we are concerned that our children should mix in their own society and find their levels there — or, in other words, struggle for power there. But our society is a big, complex phenomenon, and part of existing within it happily must be the ability to be left out of it sometimes, or to opt out of it, without embarrassment. In fact, to take a satisfying part in society we have to be able to stand apart once in a while, if only to reassess our role within it. In short, each of us must be prepared to ask the eternal question 'Who am I?', and to ask it in an empty room. Why, then, do we nag or worry the timid child, especially if the poor thing is a boy? It is not timidity that will make him miserable in the future but shame of himself for being timid and consequent distaste for his own shameful company. As long as the lone child is seen to be eager, thriving and fearless in his apartness, as long as he is not protecting a dark and shameful secret because we are too ashamed to hear it, why should we worry about him? We grant our fellow citizens the right to differences in sexual appetite, differences in appetite for food, differences in appetite for learning; we should also grant them the right to differences in their appetite for each other's company.

Children, our fellow citizens, are not evil but only inclined to be natural. There is a fair argument that we do not and cannot teach them good behaviour but only acceptable behaviour, which is, often as not, tendentious: 'Nice girls don't say, "Piss off."' 'Nice boys don't nick daddy's *Playboy*.' 'Nice boys never do *that*!' If young people do masturbate behind their closed doors, for that is apparently what their mothers and fathers assume they are doing, what the hell? We know now they are not going to go blind or

29

mad or be made unhappy by their solitary experiments — unless adults create guilt and loneliness where neither bad feeling had to be. And if the young fellow citizen is pursuing an intellectual interest of which his parents would disapprove — reading religious tracts, say, or revolutionary ones — his landlords, even though they also happen to be his parents, have no honest or moral right to stop him.

In order that they should be able to cope later with whatever portion of solitude comes their way, children ought to be given the chance to learn how to be alone, and how can they learn this except by being left alone to some degree? In our earnest desire to have no neglected children, we neglect our fellow citizens' right to solitude, and we actually contribute towards making solitude a terrifying and unwholesome prospect. 'Go to your room' should be heard in our households only as a suggestion and never as a sentence of solitary confinement.

5

Solitude:
Privation or Privilege?

...oneself is already a handful.
　　　　Arthur Koestler, 'Solitary Confinement'

The ultimate punishments delivered by most societies
today are the death penalty and solitary confinement,
and there will always be people who would choose
the first of these as the easier. To be Crusoe with no
promise of Friday, albeit fed, sheltered and even
relieved of many mundane cares, seems to many of us
literally a living death; however, there are others like
Arthur Koestler, who was a prisoner in China, to
whom solitary confinement offered the opportunity
to 'cast off layers of irrelevancy'. To be honest, most
of us think only madmen, neurotic film stars, great
sinners or saints could really 'want to be alone' or
could even bear it. In other words, it's pretty generally assumed that the condition of solitariness must
produce the bad feeling of loneliness. The 'loner'
is considered an eccentric. In the case of a little old
spinster librarian, the loner is to be pitied. In the
case of a holy hermit, he is to be held in the same
awed and bemused admiration pagans must have felt
when they saw paraded before the temples glorious

human sacrifices to their gods. Because we know from the reports of prisoners and lone survivors that enforced isolation can drive men mad, we think a man must be a little mad to want to be alone. Solitude is crazy and dangerous. 'I couldn't work alone at home the way you do,' a woman I know said the other day, echoing a comment I've heard more times than I can count. 'I just haven't got the self-discipline!' In other words, she and all the others who say this assume that if they were to work in solitude, they would fall apart, dither, disintegrate and generally behave in a loony way.

Even though solitude for any length of time is considered a dangerous condition and conducive to suicidal feelings of loneliness rigorously to be avoided, we all struggle to have that precious gift known as privacy. Virtually never, for instance, will a young married couple that has any choice in the matter live with in-laws. Even in the cities of the East, the extended family system is breaking down in large part because emancipated young women will no longer agree to accept low status in their husbands' households, but prefer to risk perilous solitude in the name of romantic love and of the privacy in which romance can flourish. In our own society, we are outraged if our letters are opened or our telephones tapped, and we do not interfere when married friends quarrel. We are shocked at newspaper reports of children sleeping three to a bed in the slums of our great cities (even though not that long ago such accommodation would have been considered generous), but at the same time we concern ourselves regularly in books and women's magazines with the plight of the only child.

We don't willingly surrender our privacy; indeed,

most people want more of it. Affluence and refinement demand privacy. The richer the man, the farther back his house is set from the run of other men (unless he is rich in New York, where 'moving up in the world' means having a penthouse). The more revered the man, the less noise others make in the corridor outside his study. But privacy also means breaking society into smaller and smaller units until each of us, like it or not, at one time or another, protracted or not, must become a unit of one. For example, the housewife not long before wedded for love is going to find herself one day living with a young child or two in a flat without resident grandparents. She will then spend 100 per cent of her waking day alone with screaming and savage company, not yet on a level of intellectual exchange, and it's no wonder she may feel rather like the Birdman of Alcatraz Prison locked up with vultures. Her husband, who has possibly never spent a day in his life coping with the mundane duties of housekeeping, has a nearly 40 per cent chance of divorcing his wife; he also stands an increasing risk of being left by her so she can go out and 'find herself'. She, if the marriage endures, stands a better than 60 per cent chance of being predeceased by her husband. If solitude really is dangerous, it seems most of us at one time or another will be in grave danger.

We can't have privacy without risking solitude. Of course, there will always be members of the *avant garde* who recommend going backwards, in this case back to versions of the extended family. Economists and sociologists can advance arguments for and against the feasibility of this, but it merely takes an interested observer of society to notice that the success of communal life, and particularly

33

of extended family life, depends upon the self-abnegation of the youngest members, particularly women. It is sad, but our devotion to the twin causes of longevity and birth control means that extended households would function chiefly as geriatric shelters, havens for the incapable and incontinent, at the great sacrifice of youthful (primarily female) hope and promise. Only if we let death and birth have their way with us again (and if, incidentally, we let nature cull the handicapped), and if we deprive women of their painful struggle towards self-expression, is it conceivable that we might return to the huge, sheltering family units of our past and to a surcease of loneliness...for some.

Except for a very few experiments, communal living in our society has come to signify failure and inadequacy. After all, don't we put our handicapped, our aged, our mad, our villainous into special communities? Primitive societies, like as not, expelled these elements from the community into death or solitary exile. For good or bad, communal living, from boarding-schools to prisons, is virtually a punishment among us. The ideal of communal living has become much less attractive too, it seems, than it was to young people of the 1960s, whose attempts at brotherly love litter Southern California with the ruins of abandoned communes.

The truth is that we are not so willing to relieve our 'existential despair' if it must be at 'some cost to personal identity, emotional intimacy and individual achievement'. For this is the price the Israeli kibbutznik paid for relief from solitude and what is commonly called loneliness, as Bruno Bettelheim, with some apparent reluctance, admits in his book *Children of the Dream*.[1] Since Bettelheim's investigation took place, the kibbutz system has changed radically. In 1980, when I paid my last visit to Israel, a kibbutznik friend took me to visit his home on the Kibbutz K'Far Blum and showed me how there, as in most of the other kibbutzim, there was increasing privacy and private ownership. I asked him if he thought the inhabitants of the kibbutz had become lonelier. 'I don't know,' he said, 'but when I was a child here we all lived together away from our parents, in dormitories. We did everything together, and if you went off alone, people wondered what was wrong with you. Lonely? I was lonely all the time. Now everything has changed. It's more like normal life.'

What is 'normal life' but the life being led by the majority in a particular group at a particular time? Israel sees herself as part of the West, and by 'normal' my kibbutznik friend meant the life of ambition, privacy, and quick gratification that we live here. For him, existence without privacy, possessions or personal pride, existence without solitude had not been 'normal', nor even in the least less lonely than life as we lead it in our separate flats, behind doors that double-lock. In other words, as he himself might have said, nothing is perfect. Furthermore, it would be hopelessly disingenuous to imagine that ambition and privacy are priorities merely for the 'privileged classes'.

I listened to an American child psychiatrist lecturing recently on the 'Disease of Loneliness' to a well-heeled audience. He advised us that a child should never sleep alone in a room, that infants should sleep with their parents and that siblings should share rooms throughout adolescence, for only such calculated destruction of solitude would 'cure' the 'sickness' of loneliness. Sitting in the front row of his audience, it is worth mentioning, and nodding approval, was a man wearing a T-shirt on which was printed Dorothy Parker's alleged epitaph: 'If you can read this, you're too close!' What the doctor was suggesting was not that his society should avoid loneliness by living in imitation of an idealized past, as experimental communes do, or even in imitation of another culture, as is done on some Hampstead *ashrams*, but that it should live in imitation of poverty. This is a 'cure' for loneliness that seems to me pretentious, dishonest and — since there is no reason to imagine that those who are overcrowded are any less lonely — totally silly.

As a community, we in the West have achieved relative affluence, and we have the attendant privacy. Without judging whether this is 'good' or 'bad', it must be clear that to try to live without the attributes of wealth and solitude, in the hope of thus alleviating our loneliness, would be unworthy, undignified and, since loneliness is not actually the product of wealth or solitude, probably unsuccessful. Surely, what we must try to do is to learn how to make what we can of what we have the fortune to possess. Making the most of something — even privacy and wealth — may well mean sharing it, but do we really imagine that anyone gains if we destroy it?

Even if we make the dubious assumption that the majority of those who used to live in our extended families were never lonely, we still cannot go backwards to Victorian days and before. We've never gone backwards successfully except when cataclysm drove us back, and then we made good our losses as fast as we could. I've spoken to many

36

people who recall the sense of love and community during the London Blitz, but I've yet to meet anyone who would have had the Blitz continue at the price that was being paid. We seem bound to acquire more leisure, whether it be the leisure of affluence or of unemployment (a condition no longer synonymous with impecunity and starvation). The letters that come to an agony aunt about unemployment — and they are numerous — are concerned not with making ends meet but with restlessness and frustration. We are probably going to live longer and to continue divorcing, shifting and splitting the family unit. Microchip technology is bound someday to reduce work teams and to isolate their members. In other words, like it or not, there is going to be more solitude, and if we cannot accept it or function within it, if we immediately cry 'loneliness', then there is going to be more pain in life for us than ever before.

We will not conquer our fear of solitude by learning to need each other more, a fatuous sentiment attuned to juke-boxes of the 1950s, but by learning how to do without each other for long periods of time. People who need people will most certainly not be the luckiest people in the world, and I find it hard to believe they ever were. Take the widow, for example, who has not had a holiday in all the years since her husband's death for the simple reason that she cannot imagine travelling alone. The genteel agoraphobia that strikes so many single people creates the pain of loneliness in their solitude. Or what about the student at university who is so unaccustomed to coping without people around him that he actually prefers failure to remaining alone? And we cannot ignore that very dangerous 'needer of people' who will espouse any cause, accept any prejudice and join any army just as long as it prevents him from being alone. Is there really any reason to imagine that we cannot help each other more, or love each other more, by needing each other less? After all, if we are ever to find sense in the way we love, it must lie not in loving the people we cannot live without but in loving the people with whom we can live.

There used to be American Indian tribes that sent their young men out to live alone for a considerable time in the wilderness as part of their initiation into adulthood. It was important that the young braves should learn to master the tools of survival they would need on long hunting trails, but it was also imperative that each man should come to terms with his own personality and his own nightmares in order that he could work alone and sustain himself alone. Only the man who was able to survive alone was considered able to work harmoniously within adult society. In other words, only the man who did not strictly need people, whatever his preference, could be one of the people. The wilderness in our lives is of a different variety: we find our food in supermarkets and not in streams; we have put our God into cathedrals, not into a fox or a tree. We are rarely physically alone in our wilderness, and yet we shrivel with horror at the prospect of loneliness if we have not developed solitary tools. We need patience, as the Indian did, but we need compassion too, which he did not, for in our wilderness we are perpetually jostled by strangers. We need a sense of humour. All these qualities and others which we need for successful survival amount to independence: the ability to function alone with some degree of efficiency and even of cheerfulness.

Is independence a selfish condition? I don't think it is. It is the dependent person who sees others as a prop to his ego and a solace to his pain, who, in other words, does not see others at all. What is more selfish, and actually more lonely by any standard, than the inability to see and recognize other people? Independence is developed by observing, by thinking and by making discoveries in solitude — including discoveries as mundane as that of the man who finds that he can darn his own socks or the woman who discovers that she really can mend a fuse. It seems a shame that our society cannot enforce a period of aloneness in every young person's life, a period when he, like the Indian initiate, is thrown on his own company, albeit within our busy wilderness. Deliberately to close a door and survey with curiosity the nature of aloneness can be enlightening and strengthening.

Nevertheless, on the basis of my own observation and letters I receive, I must conclude that this experience of aloneness is precisely what most people most desperately fear. At the first tingle of anxiety in the silence of the room, we turn on the television, play a record we do not hear, switch on the radio, do something — anything — that will grant us at least a fantasy of company. We even fall in love and marry unwisely out of fear of loneliness, and continue affairs that have little joy in them. Or we ring for someone — anyone — to join us and dispel the threat of solitude, even if the visitor replaces it with boredom. Or we drink too much. Or we eat too much. And whatever we do too much, or take too much, is not enough. We're still afraid.

6

Missions of Discovery

> [Shame]…is a shameful apprehension of something and this something is me. I am ashamed of what I *am*. Through shame I have discovered an aspect of my being. Yet…shame is not originally a phenomenon of reflection. In fact no matter what results one can obtain in solitude by the religious practice of shame, it is in its primary structure shame before somebody….
>
> Jean-Paul Sartre, *Being and Nothingness*

Shame is the shuddering that results from feeling that others are thinking badly of us or laughing at us. Solitude is frightening because of our unfamiliarity with it; and because it demands to be filled, it smacks of loss. And solitude is shameful because we think others assume that we could not have chosen freely our detestable condition of aloneness but we have been thrust into it because nobody likes us enough to stay with us or even to join us. The opposite of solitude for most people is 'popularity' Shame turns human beings into sentient objects, like hospital patients or prisoners who have been publicly weighed and found light or flawed. The man alone thinks others must believe he is not worth very much, or wouldn't someone have claimed his company? And if he has not freed his own opinions from the opinions of others — if he is not in some measure independent — then he must begin to think he really could not be worth very much, or how could all the others allow him to be alone? This giddy and unappetizing spiral means the man alone, persuaded he is not worth very much because he is being left alone, can have nothing but contempt for the person who does offer to dispel his loneliness. After all, if he's been left alone because he's worthless, then anyone who actually chooses to keep him company must not be worth enough to find someone better than he.

Furthermore, shame soon becomes a fixed emotion and unyielding to reason. How many times have I assured women who are ashamed to go out because of, say, the length of a nose or the flatness of a chest that a million other longer-nosed, flatter women are happy? Yet I know most of those who write to me with such problems persist in their blind humiliation. Show a man proof that he is not by a long shot the only person whose sex life is less than flourishing and he, in a kind of exaltation of shame, will reject the evidence. The folly of shame about aloneness is nowhere more apparent than among the young. Anyone who has counselled teenagers, for example, knows that girls often find themselves pregnant after an encounter they did not relish and for which they were not prepared, but which took place because they preferred the risk of unwanted pregnancy to the humiliation of being jilted or being seen to be alone. Before there were cinemas and discothèques and other forms of unchaperoned entertainment for the young, in the days when maiden aunts were surrounded by children,

41

albeit not of their own making, and nice girls were rarely alone with nice boys (rather more frequently, perhaps, with cads), in those days shame fell on the girl who went out and did 'it', not the girl who stayed at home alone and didn't. Well, we cannot and would not return to those days, any more than we would return to bustles and snuff; however, in providing unmarried people with a modern, unsupervised carnival of courtship, we have also created the shame of being uninvited, unable or just unwilling to join it. This shameful solitude of the unpartnered, at home alone on the 'loneliest night of the week', is felt also by older divorced people, widowed people and by a lot of married people.

It is ironical that a society such as ours, in which solitary people feel ashamed of being at home, unrung, unloved, unchosen, is the first to allow a single woman into virtually any entertainment unescorted, without anyone noticing or giving much of a damn. In the not very distant past, right up to the flaming twenties and beyond for most levels of society, a nice young woman was not welcome without an escort at the theatre or the opera; she could not go alone in the streets. Until the 1960s in New York City there were numerous cocktail lounges and restaurants where a woman alone would not be served and where two women or a party of them were forbidden to sit at the bar. In London there is still one hostelry and a few private clubs that refuse admission or service to women on their own, but as both management and clientele of these establishments are getting long in the tooth, these quaint restrictions will soon be lifted, in the natural course of things. Most public places are genuinely public and permitted to single people, yet rarely do the unescorted enter them alone.

The impropriety of being alone in a happy crowd of couples or friends is lodged within individual men and women, as is the shame of being at home alone.

Shame is a reaction to the response of others to us, yes, but it can also be a reaction to what we *imagine* is the response of others. The lonely person sweats at the very thought that others will think he is too dull, or too weird, or too ugly to get anyone to agree to be with him, and the lone woman in a restaurant blushes behind her menu at the notion that others will think she is a dish that's gone off; but the fact is others are much too busy thinking about themselves and the impression they are making to feel concern for the condition of anyone else. If shame in loneness, and shyness, seem related to immature narcissism – 'Everyone is looking at *me*. Everyone is laughing at *me*. Everyone is noticing *me*' – then society is composed largely of immature narcissists who are much, much too self-absorbed to worry about why a strange woman is dining alone in a restaurant or how a bachelor dares to arrive solitary at a concert. Oddly enough, narcissism and the horror of loneliness are closely connected: if we all became capable of going out in public truly in order to experience rather than in order to be experienced or to be seen to be experiencing, we would have to notice each other more, and therefore we would actually become less isolated in our loneliness.

Reluctant though I've learned to be to jar the hornets' nest, I will have to say here that the shame of loneliness carries a sexual burden, as does much of human shame. When the mother of a 16-year-old boy worries about what he is doing upstairs in his room all by himself, and suspects she knows what he's doing up there, she's probably quite right to suspect, although she is silly to worry. (Since one demand of the new feminism is an equal appetite for masturbation, I'll grant a mother might be quite correct about her teenaged daughter too, even though, in my honest opinion, the girl is probably reading a novel or tweezing her eyebrows.)

What do people on their own do for sex? Presumably, the best they can. Therefore, the shame of loneness among the unattached includes the shame of being suspected of having no sex life at all — what a horrifying fate! — or of masturbation, which, despite its condescending endorsement by noted 'sexologists', is still considered by most people to be naughty, antisocial, irreligious, pathetic or just comical. 'Why do people masturbate?' asks the dim-witted innocent who poses all the questions in David Reuben's *Everything You Always Wanted to Know About Sex*. 'The primary reason,' replies the jocular know-it-all 'is masturbation is fun. Certainly,' he continues quickly, 'not as much fun as fully-fledged sexual intercourse, but the next thing to it.'

In other words, masturbation is a private confession that no partner has volunteered or been seduced into the better game. Masturbation is the 'next thing' to fully-fledged sex and therefore only a notch above nothing at all. To masturbate is to be as the driver whose car breaks down in the desert and who finally drains his own radiator and survives on the brackish liquid. Is it not shameful to exist alone in a sexual desert while everybody else is splashing around naked in the swim?

Since there is every chance that the lone person does masturbate at least as much as the person who is not alone, and an even better chance that he used to masturbate in the suspect solitude of his teenaged

44

bedroom, and since he himself agrees with the consensus that considers masturbation a sorry and pathetic little practice, or even with the maternal opinion that it is wicked, in his own estimation he has reason to be ashamed. Among women, who were not until recently supposed to enjoy sex at all, shame about solitary pleasures has always been particularly marked. In his book *Sex*, under the section entitled 'Masturbation', Dr Michael Carrera tells us that 58 per cent of the women whom Kinsey canvassed in the 1940s masturbated but 82 per cent of those recently polled by the indefatigable Shere Hite masturbate. These figures suggest to the doctor that more women masturbate in liberation than ever before. To me they suggest that more women admit to doing it.

How do we teach ourselves not to be ashamed when there is no justification for shame? How do we educate our emotions? There is no justification for shame in being alone; on the contrary, there may be some cause for pride. In the realm of feelings it seems we can learn only from experience. This is not to say we *do* learn from experience, only that those who want to *can* learn from experience. Knowledge increases the risk of loneliness, and as knowledge is responsibility, there will always be those who do not choose to acquire it. Like any other learning, we have to want the education of our emotions in order to receive it. Just try teaching anyone anything he does not want to learn, and you must fail. Each time we fall in love, for example, the passion can be tempered by experience (which does not, by the way, make it less satisfying — on the contrary), unless we are hooked on the passion itself rather than on its object, in which case each succeeding love will have to be a little more dramatic, traumatic and ill-starred than its predecessor, for isn't it in the nature of any drug that the dosage must increase in order to remain effective? In the same way, a sportsman addicted to the adrenalin of the ski-jump must climb higher and higher to keep the excitement going, at least until his body gives out and he gets too old for the game.

Each time we fear some exploit, the intensity of that fear diminishes with repetition. Ask anyone who has learned to drive, or to speak in public, or to cook a perfect soufflé for hungry diners. Of course, there are some physically dangerous activities like Russian roulette, where the repetition of the action would diminish the fear, except the shortening odds engender more of it. Going out alone to a movie or a meal is not really in this class of risk, but it is absolutely true that each time we allow ourselves to be seen alone (should anyone care to look) and survive the experience, we feel that much less shame. There is simply no other way to control shame except to diminish it by repetition. We can't learn from example, for nobody feels precisely as we do, and we can't learn rules to govern emotions that are by nature unruly. If fear of solitude can be dispelled by summoning courage to face it first and eventually to face it down, then the shame of being alone can be dispelled in the same way. Nor does it hurt to add a pinch of indignation: why the hell should a man or a woman alone not attend a cinema, or a concert, or a theatre, or a football match? Show me a statute on any book that forbids entertainment, music and beauty to the unattached. Why in blazes should anyone in cities as lavish in entertainment as ours be bored, frustrated or ashamed at being home alone?

'I wouldn't enjoy myself going out on my own,' says the stay-at-home (who, it so happens, has never tried to enjoy himself going out on his own but has preferred to suffer alone at home). 'I'd feel peculiar.' Maybe the first time, yes, but after that being alone in public becomes tolerable, and not long after that it becomes enjoyable, and after a little longer, for some of us, it will always be preferable to go alone than to go in dull company. For a very, very few it will always be preferable to go alone than to go in any company. This last group includes those who have learned to love a form of entertainment or art deeply and prefer to enjoy it without distraction. Is this attitude any more 'pseud' or affected than that of a self-avowed music-lover, say, too embarrassed to attend a concert because he is on his own?

Don't imagine I'm pretending that our world is established for the single person because I know it is not, having spent a large part of my own life single within it. A little anarchy in the soul of a single person helps to upset conventions and allay prejudices. Loneness and misery are concomitant only when the lone person has developed no skills of independence and is still waiting, like baby Narcissus, to be given by someone else what he can perfectly well cultivate for himself: interests, experiences and a share of happiness.

Any one of us, for any reason including chance, may spend a large part of life or almost all of life without a mate or companions. To prepare for such a possibility could be considered pessimistic, but to be prepared for it, should it arise, must be considered wise. It is wise and advisable for even the most gregarious and popular of us to learn not only that there is no shame attached to being alone or to being seen

47

to be alone, but also that there is a peculiar clarity to impressions received by the lone observer. So peculiar and so clear are they, they can sometimes seem the only impressions that are experienced totally. The presence of another, however much joy it gives, takes the edge off concentration.

> So only I was left, like Ishmael....It was cold in this dismal place....But I also thought: 'It's perfect.' If one of the objects of travel was to give yourself the explorer's thrill that you were alone...embarked on a solitary mission of discovery...then I had accomplished the traveller's dream...In the best travel books the word *alone* is implied....[2]

Implicit in these words, written by one of our wittiest and brightest travellers, is the difference between adventure and holiday, between meditation and observation, between passion and a good suntan.

It's only by having learned that he can be alone without fear or shame that any of us can be sure he truly loves the company he is keeping.

7

Accursed Activity

Though gay companions o'er the bowl
Dispel awhile the sense of ill:
Though pleasure fires the maddening soul,
The heart, — the heart is lonely still!
  Lord Byron, 'One Struggle More and I am Free'

The space within that we call loneliness is sometimes the size of a nutshell and sometimes vaulted and echoing. There are many shy, lonely people sitting in their own rooms like cells locked from the inside; but there are also expressions of loneliness other than the silent, isolated one. Many people, also in flight from loneliness and shame, scurry like medieval courtiers trying to flee the plague already lodged in their bloodstreams. This flight from loneliness leads us not just to stultifying relationships but also to addictions: to promiscuity, to drugs, to drinks, to over-spending, to over-eating, to gambling, to febrile ambition, and to compulsive, foolish, even criminal behaviour. A London newspaper recently ran interviews with unmarried teenaged schoolgirls who had deliberately become pregnant and borne the children of passing lovers because, each girl said in her own way, they wanted something of their own, something to love them, something they could love, something to keep them company. Can anyone imagine anything more careless of the future than such a remedy for current loneliness? Isn't it like requesting a guillotine to cure hay fever?

Anyone who sees loneliness as a disease must imagine the disease has a cure, yet haven't we learned that every cure has side-effects, and virtually any cure can become the very disease it was taken to alleviate? A junkie, for instance, driven to addiction by psychic pain, is destined to discover that the drug he welcomed at first as a 'cure' because it made him 'feel better' (which, by the way, is not precisely what a cure should do), has insidiously become alienation, loneliness and humiliation. Soon for him there may be no way forward to a 'cure' and no way back to the original malady, but only a pervasive and squalid despair which he cannot escape. Hence the daunting difficulty of treating those addicted to drugs or encouraging them to treat themselves: the way back is sleepless sorrow; the way forward is sorrow punctuated by unconsciousness which is nothing but loss of self, which, in turn, is a pretty fair definition of real, burning loneliness. Moreover, for brief periods, drugs, drink, gambling and certain sexual appetites grant an illusion of society and brotherhood, of a league against loneliness. This bond among addicts, however, *is* only an illusion, for it is devoted to oblivion, and oblivion comes to each of us separately. Even lovers who fall asleep at the same moment, or those who raise and touch their cups of cyanide, part at the threshold to darkness. We can share a lot with other people, but not nothing.

Sexual promiscuity is flight from loneliness of another kind, and an especially poignant one, because its moments of oblivion depend upon the presence and attention of another person. The act of love can be seen as a triumph of irony, leading its participants — be they old friends or new ones — to a deceptive climax of togetherness, which is actually experienced quite separately, and returning them both to the arms of a stranger. Thus two people can use each other to provide momentary oblivion from loneliness without even knowing each other's names. One of Boccacio's naughty monks called sexual intercourse 'putting the Devil in Hell' but for most of us it is more a matter of trying to put Adam and Eve together again. If the act of love is seen as a metaphor for mankind's desire to join hands and rush back to Paradise where there is no loneliness, no separateness, no dread, then we must admit that man does not have Heaven's gift for making surcease of loneliness permanent. Furthermore, when it ends, each moment in our specious Eden recreates and increases the agony of exile. Promiscuity is generally accepted now as expressive of emotional or physical frigidity, and the sexually promiscuous individual, like the junkie, takes small joy in his drug beyond the alleviation of his terror of being caught short without it. If the sexually promiscuous actually savour their forays into Paradise, how can they bear to return so frequently and so relentlessly to a bedsitter in the Earls Court Road?

No, excess does not relieve loneliness; on the contrary, the remorse that is part of every hangover after any excess is a condition that is like shame, a condition that becomes a factor of loneliness. When the solitary remorse is too keen to bear, it drives us back into the oblivion of excess, which is followed by the agony of remorse. And so it goes: addiction is an unappetising round of excess and remorse, oblivion and pain, leading to nothing at all but the degradation and final sentencing of a lonely soul to solitary confinement within a decrepit self.

Drink, sex, gambling, drugs, food — all release the thrills of specific juices in the body, and at various times they can all be pleasures. To shun all pleasure for fear of losing self is just as indicative of distress as is losing oneself in excess of pleasure and thereby, incidentally, losing the pleasure — for what can please a lost self? People who are excessive in their embraces, their calories, their jolts of adrenalin or heroin rarely present our society with anything but trouble. Fluent celebrations of excess have been presented by William Burroughs, Malcolm Lowry, Jean Genet, the Marquis de Sade and others of cirrhotic or erotic temper, but the vast majority of those who try to 'cure' their loneliness or any other pain through addiction sink without ever having made a statement.

Nevertheless, excess is an experiment that all curious and intelligent people will make in their lives: it is necessary to have too much sometimes in order to understand an experience, or to enjoy it, or to learn our own limits, or even to exercise the equipment of satisfaction. Anyone who lives without ever trying too much of something must be leading a dry and pinched existence; and no doubt there are people who live fully by having too much of a lot of things a lot of the time. However, there is a point where each of us begins to have too much of too much, where we spin out of control and become addicts in flight (like as not from loneliness) and victims of our own excess. Those of us who have had contact with compulsive eaters (usually women), for instance, know the great difference between someone who likes her food a lot, and likes a lot of it, and someone who eats compulsively although food has actually become her poison, so as she eats it, she hates it and hates herself for eating it. As with the food addict, so with the alcoholic, the junkie, the gambler and, most tragically, because it is such a cruel travesty, with the compulsive lover.

The flight from loneliness can also lead to a life of astonishing activity that can benefit the man leading it without in the least alleviating his loneliness: 'in this accursedly active and even more accursedly *restless* life of mine,' the impresario Alexander Korda wrote to his nephew, Michael, 'you can imagine in what loneliness I'm living....'[1]

Korda was a rich, influential, self-made man who led a life of fabulous glamour, who never had to be alone in a room unless he chose to be, never had to be alone in bed, never had to be alone at table. He had, like many celebrated men, to fight so hard for privacy and solitude that it began to seem to him that if people would only leave him more alone, he might be much less lonely. However, readers of his nephew's interesting biography will see that Korda created for himself a lonely life which was 'accursedly active' in its flight from loneliness. As in the case of the lives of some rulers and many celebrated entertainers, to say nothing of those of politicians, practically from childhood Korda expended all his energy to create of himself a man to be respected, admired, perhaps loved, feared, worshipped by a large audience: a famous man who would seem to have no occasion to be lonely. Yet what cliché, spoken or revealed, rises from envied and glamorous figures like Korda, Marilyn Monroe, Princess Margaret, Elvis Presley? 'It's lonely at the top. Won't someone love me for myself?' But who is the 'self' underneath the ballyhoo? Such lives of daunting activity and stupendous trivia are led in flight from loneliness, and since loneliness is a private, inner feeling, that has got to mean they are led in flight from self. They are lives not of discovery but of invention. They are wind-up, clockwork lives for the most part, and in the end they are often lives to rent. It cannot be in losing self that one overcomes the pain of loneliness. The pain of loneliness is already the pain of loss.

The flight from loneliness is often evident in deeds and words of glamorous figures, but loneliness itself is also frequently the theme of those who have created brilliant works of art. In the letters of Vincent Van Gogh, for instance, the journals of Kafka, the diary of Virginia Woolf, loneliness is always there or nearby: be it the loneliness of isolation, or the loneliness of madness, or the loneliness of possessing a truth with which the whole world seems to disagree. Masterpieces upon which mankind prides itself are born of compulsion, sometimes of terror, of excess of feeling, of painstaking patience, always of the exploration of separateness. A great work of art has got to be the product of consciousness; it is the very emblem of consciousness. A great artist participates in feeling rather than opinion, action rather than distraction, technique rather than knowledge, and truth rather than happiness. When he is working, the artist must be an impassioned solitary. He is not in flight from loneliness, although he may hate it, but he is an explorer of loneliness and he suffers for it, be it in a way that many of us might envy. 'The poet skims off the best of life and puts it in his work,' Leo Tolstoy wrote in a notebook he kept while he was writing *War and Peace*. 'That is why his work is beautiful and his life is bad.'[2]

Few of us can, or would even dare to, penetrate as deeply as the artist must into the kingdom of feeling, and yet we can benefit from allowing ourselves to stand at the border of that ardent loneliness, without opinion and without knowledge, and permit the works of artists to help us do the single thing each of us can do only for himself: feel — and, if we must, feel loneliness.

8

A Slight Insanity

I have never felt lonesome or in the least opressed
by a sense of solitude, but once, and that was a
few weeks after I came to [live alone in] the
woods, when, for an hour, I doubted if the near
neighborhood of man was not essential to a
serene and healthy life. To be alone was something unpleasant. But I was at the same time
conscious of a slight insanity in my mood, and
seemed to foresee my recovery. In the midst of
a gentle rain while these thoughts prevailed, I
was suddenly sensible of such sweet and benefi-
cent society in Nature…as made the fancied
advantages of human neighborhood insignificant,
and I have never thought of them since….

Henry David Thoreau, *Walden*

There are special conditions that make ours a lonely
society — not a 'bad' society, or a 'wrong' society,
for being 'good' and being 'right' no more end loneliness than being 'bad' and being 'wrong' create it —
simply a lonely society. One of these conditions is
that our society, and therefore each of us within
it, has lost touch with nature. The young man on
roller-skates gliding through a crowd he doesn't see,

surrounded by voices, traffic noises, warnings, jokes, wisdom and foolishness he can't hear because a pocket tape-recorder is plugged into his distracted mind, is an apt symbol of our time and of our loneliness.

Because we rarely listen to silence, we are forgetting the signals that filled primeval stillness. It isn't often birdsong that awakens most of us nowadays, but probably a pneumatic drill outside the window, or the manic glee of an early morning disc-jockey on the clock radio, or the coughing of a heavy smoker in the neighbouring flat. The changing wind means less to us than a television weather forecast; even though the wind is more reliable, we've stopped hearing it. We receive our messages *en masse* and not as a personal bulletin from nature. We have become addicts and generators of noise. When we visit our seasides we carry along radios and tape-recorders against the deprivation of racket, just as prudent desert travellers take canteens of water. Our trite melodies rise up over the swell of the sea and the rattle of pebbles drawn back against the sand. Reading and writing are perhaps the last of our activities to be undertaken — when they are undertaken seriously — alone and in silence; and it seems that as we hear more of the ephemeral broadcast word, we read less. Only look at the financial reports of most publishing companies and the literary quality of our bestsellers to be convinced that some day it may be everywhere as it already appears to be in Southern California: reading will become an activity considered marginally more sustaining than chewing gum.

We are increasingly alienated from the sounds and the textures of the planet we inhabit. Year in and year out few of us walk barefoot over earth, or meet any fellow animals except our domestic pets, or hear the sea, or eat a fruit not weighed out by the pound, or walk by ourselves alone in nature's witty silence. The more distanced we become from our birthplace, the more we fear its silences and its wildernesses, even its beauties. A man who will take his life in his hands, hurling himself along a motorway between two big cities, would be distressed, even terrified, to find himself alone under the branches of a forest. The truth is, most of us urban and suburban folk know a lot more these days about how to survive a nuclear holocaust than we do about how to survive in the quiet, ancient wildernesses of our homelands.

Living on a planet we have not only ceased to love but, it almost seems, even ceased to need except as a platform to hold us up in space, having lost the personal, respectful relationship of our ancestors with Earth, would be less conducive to that loss and homesickness we call loneliness if we had replaced nature with an exquisite, understandable culture. But we have become visitors from outer space on our own turf. Very few of us understand all the workings of our intricate machines, or see through all the ambiguities of governments that court votes in a straight line and then follow a crooked one when they are in power, or comprehend the logic of profit that flourishes on poverty. There even seems to be a mystique of technology which laymen are not encouraged to penetrate and each new machine creates a new jargon, another set of experts and another set of fools. Contemplation of mortality is discouraged by tunes set against the take-offs and landings of aircraft. In New York City's skyscrapers passengers in lifts are regaled by piped-in romantic and patriotic ballads, presumably to prevent them from thinking what a frightening, and demeaning, and unnatural thing it is to stand in a box hurtling towards the top of a building too high to climb on foot. There is an increasing confusion between consumer durables and emotions; thus ads on American TV can ask 'Have you hugged your child today?', as if love were a manufactured commodity.

We are really out of touch with the nature that Thoreau and other transcendentalists, poets, philosophers, farmers, wonderful idealists like William Cobbett (who wrote in *Cottage Economy* 'a couple of flitches of bacon are worth fifty thousand Methodist sermons and religious tracts…they are great softeners of the temper and promoters of domestic harmony') and generations of country people have cherished; and rarely, by the way, have they complained of loneliness. We have lost our way in great urban sprawls, where we live in houses we would not know how to build ourselves (and might not want to), where we often work at jobs without wholly understanding them, and where most labour produces an abstract yield that is quite inedible. Moreover, a lot of us never handle raw materials but only the frozen dinner, the baked bread, the made garment, the woven cloth. Most important, we live in a world where, for the first time, many of us must remain absolutely unaware of nature's majesty and transcendent beauty, where the six o'clock news has replaced sunset, and the religious epilogue does the job that once was done by the night sky. These are all components of the loss that makes us lonely.

Of course, we have been freed by technology from the vagaries of weather and crops. We can now watch the stock market with more interest than the barometer, and in our society we probably won't starve. We can value a man much more for what he says than for what he does, and we remain young for a long time. We have infinitely more time than ever we did in the days when each of us devoted most of his life to staying alive. Moreover, this new control of the physical world, combined with no notable increase of self-control, also means we can do ourselves in more efficiently than ever before. What do we free all our time for? What do we do with it? Mostly, it seems to me, we try to kill it — 'as if you could kill time,' Thoreau writes in *Walden*, 'without injuring eternity'.

It is our attempt to fill the significant silence with banal noises that makes us lonely. It is the loss of our human need to survive — each of us and all together — from the land, and it is our new need, unforeseen by the ancient sages, to make each individual, catered existence 'deeply meaningful' apart from all other existences that makes us lonely. Once, to survive was purpose enough, and praise was given to God for the opportunity; now, however, survival goes pretty much without saying, and we want more: we want to be happy, and that means we do not want to be lonely. Yet, what is potentially more lonely than countless seekers of individual identity squabbling over steam-heated, air-conditioned space, and isolated from the planet on which they live, careless of her bounty and ignorant of her might?

With the loss of Eden, Adam and Eve lost dominion over nature; that is, they lost their natural place. Whether it was the fall from Paradise or the invention of the cotton gin, the end result is with us now: we have been wrenched from nature. We have become inept and fastidious. Nor is it merely a matter of not knowing any longer how to build a lean-to or skin a

60

rabbit. About ten years ago mothers and mothers-to-be all over the Western world began a small but organized and articulate revolution against modern methods of battery birthing in hospitals and in favour of what is called 'natural childbirth'. Childbed deaths and infant mortality have been greatly reduced, true, but new mothers were finding that superfluous anaesthetics and the zealous detachment of highly trained obstetricians were separating them from the experience of giving birth and turning love into an afterthought, often long postponed. Technology was increasing alienation — even creating it — in the last place it would be expected: between mother and newborn baby.

Living here on a planet that has become mysterious, even fantastic, surrounded by incredible objects and jostled by other human beings whose behaviour is often inconsistent and alarming, we make a plea for happiness and significance. However, because we are out of touch with nature and removed from faith, we have to look towards supernature, as advocated by doctors, gurus, charlatans, therapists, sociologists, psychologists and even agony aunts. But there is no magician and no magical help to restore our broken contact with the natural world. If we want it back, one way or another, we will have to work for it.

Mind you, however negligent we are of nature, she reclaims us in due course. In the end she prevails. Even were a man to sit perfectly still, alone, unthinking, he would be subject to those compulsions of heart and bowels that put kings in their places: he would breathe; he would hunger; and, in due course, he would die. Nature works. Nature is action, and action, voluntary or involuntary, makes us part of nature. The actions of nature are purposeful, and human action seems most natural when it too is purposeful. Once, when survival was the purpose of most action, no tribesman thought twice about what he was doing here: he was hunting, building, appeasing with song, prayer and sacrifice; he was hanging on to precarious life as hard as he could. Do you imagine that he was lonely? And later, when praise of God became our very purpose, no one questioned what he was doing here: he was here in obedience to God's will, just as other creatures were, and he was here to perform God's will. Whatever miseries he suffered, it's hard to believe he complained of loneliness. But what is our purpose now?

To ease loneliness, each of us must look for purpose, for it is purpose that returns us to nature. For some of us nature herself is still the purpose, whether she takes the form of an old-age pensioner's allotment or a wind-swept island in the Outer Hebrides. People really do find necessary solace in growing things or merely in walking among growing things. We know, for example, that the failure of urban architecture of the 1960s came about partly because the high-rise block removed tenants with a garden tradition too far from the earth. In Manhattan, where people are accustomed to living in towering boxes, it is a rare apartment that has no greenery, and pot plants are sold in fashionable boutiques, on street corners and even in the depths of the subway. In the mid-1960s a book called *How to Grow Your Own Avocado* was a local bestseller. I noticed on a recent trip that the avocado, not a very lush or pretty plant, has been replaced by homegrown pineapples and other exotic flora, but it remains true that few Manhattan cliff-dwellers are content without some living or growing thing that needs them. A more recent American bestseller called *Living Alone and Liking It*,[1] along with advice about how to sauté a half-breast of turkey for one, gives us the information that the author was cured of her own loneliness by growing patio tomatoes. From the time I brought the baby plants home,' writes Lynn Shahan, 'I was totally engrossed in a very rewarding pastime.' There are plenty of worse ways to enliven solitude!

Not all of us like animals or have green thumbs; a lot of us suffer from hay fever, and we can't all find sense in raising plants (just as many of us fail to find sense in raising children). So we must each actively hunt for our purpose, since our basic one — to survive here — has been taken away from us by more efficient machines. To repair our rift from Earth, we must discover a reason to be here — create our reason, if need be — and fill that empty space within where nature would have us purposeful.

What should a man's purpose be? Miss Shahan, in her friendly and cosy book, suggests everything from hooking rugs to cooking gourmet meals for one. I dare say she, like me, knew that what her readers had come to her for was to be told how to survive loneliness and she, like me, did not really know what to tell them. I don't believe any one of us can tell another what his purpose should be, or even what it could be. I for one see no purpose at all in team sport, for example, but I've met men and women who could not live without it and who have no space left for loneliness. It seems to me our most natural purpose is in some way to advance our society: our purpose is functional, I think, and involves giving of ourselves to life. More than that, I cannot tell you. How frustrating this must be for the people who still want a magic 'cure'! Yet I cannot honestly do better than to say that each man appears to be most natural and comfortable, and least lonely in nature, when he is standing up and stretching for something he can't quite reach.

9

Faith or Fellowship

> When Rabbi Yitzhak Meir was a little boy his
> mother once took him to see the maggid of
> Koznitz. There someone said to him: 'Yitzhak
> Meir, I'll give you a gulden if you tell me where
> God lives!' He replied: 'And I'll give you two
> gulden if you tell me where he doesn't!'
>
> Martin Buber,
> *Tales of the Hasidim: the Later Masters*

When Adam and Eve were booted out of the Garden,
they found themselves deprived of status within
nature, of comfort between themselves, of comfort
each with himself, of eternal life (and therefore the
ability to endure without progeny) and, if not of
God himself or of His love, then at least of God's
undivided attention. Ever since that Exile — or, as
some see it, ever after the expulsion from soft darkness into hard consciousness — we have clamoured
to catch God's ear but without much success. As a
matter of fact, our noise, raised hopefully towards
Heaven, seems as often as not to wake the devil.
Nevertheless, one fact is apparent in most religious
tracts and confessions: those men who find God
within themselves, around themselves, everywhere,

never complain of loneliness. Therefore it seems reasonable to conclude that a society like ours, which complains bitterly of loneliness, has lost God.

There is in all of us the need for some sort of transcending spiritual involvement with space beyond what we know and with life beyond what we live. This is a generalization that I don't think anyone could criticize or gainsay. Our spiritual need is based upon questions: why are we here? What is our inspiration? Why must we die? Even if we would prefer these great mysteries to go away, they are abiding, and it is we who are just passing through. It is these formidable questions that make us small, vulnerable; and because no reply to them is heard, these are the questions that make us lonely, especially before dawn or in the late afternoon, when clinical depression is most likely to strike and when we are too weary to outrun the perplexities of our existence.

Certainly, the most comforting and convenient thing to do is to throw the mysteries back at God and to call them His will. God stands between believers and themselves, a cosmic ear to intercept the internal dialogue, a divine explanation for the eternal questions, and a conscience. If God is there for him, a man cannot be lonely; he cannot even be alone, for he believes a bit of God lives within himself. The very anchorite who meditates in isolation is not out of God's presence and can always be hopeful of attracting His personal attention. To love God is to have what Augustine in his *Confessions* called 'the light, melody, fragrance, mean, embracement of my inner man'. To love God is to have oneself and to offer oneself up; it is to have purpose.

Even for a man of simple faith and less elegant style than St Augustine, religion — not necessarily

Christianity — may be only a refinement of super-stition, but it is nevertheless central to his existence. A woman rubbing butter on the monkey idol in a Madrasi temple has appeased her conscience and dis-covered her purpose as surely as any saint has. These cannot be lonely people, for they are perpetually in the care and company of a presence greater than themselves. The more ecstatic their belief, it seems, the likelier it is that the mighty presence will be revealed in an idol or a vision or a relic, manifesta-tions which offer not only consolation but also something concrete to carry into solitude.

God makes good company. Proselytizers in our society have not missed the significant connection between loss of Him and ubiquitous loneliness. Missionaries to West London for example, where I happen to live, periodically push God's word (or at least his telephone number) through our letter boxes, printed on leaflets written to catch the attention of lonely people. 'God loves you and has a wonderful plan for your life!' says one of these. 'In the world's eyes you're just a statistic, a number, one person among 5,000,000,000. BUT GOD KNOWS YOU BY NAME!' Another leaflet shows a hand holding up the receiver of a telephone: 'IT'S FOR YOU' reads the headline, and the text continues, 'Someone's been trying to call you.... Jesus is calling, and the message is very simple — God loves YOU! He cares for YOU!' The appeal of such messages is to someone who lives in one of the numerous bedsitters of the area and who hears the pay-phone ring in the hall but never for him, or to an unwed mother at home all day, isolated with a baby, or to the many aged who are alone but for the woman who delivers meals-on-wheels. No doubt, many without the faith that creates saints, and even without any particular personal calling from God, run to religion for the fellowship offered.

However, for the most part our society is without belief in the abiding presence of an Almighty reigning over us who are minions of His conscience. Church-goers are not in the majority among us, and even among those who attend church the elected believer who is physically, spiritually and intellectually devoted to communion with a supernal power is probably pretty damned uncommon. Thus most of us nowa-days do without the sociability of church attendance, as well as without God as conscience, stern friend and omniscient presence.

Clearly, only a very stupid person would court loneliness by actually choosing to be without the eternal company of God. But so exacting are God's cults that a person whose election to one of them has not been signified by a mysterious predisposition cannot elect to join in truth, and if he should join in falsehood, he is going to be uncommonly lonely. In other words, atheism is as ineluctable for me and others as faith is for some. Not by a long shot is the atheist necessarily any more lonely or any less spiritual than the believer. God is but one way of satisfying spiritual needs. Thank God, there are others. Without answering all the great questions, or even any one of them, an ecstatic assault upon them can be made intellectually without faith; someone like Bertrand Russell, a thinking atheist, for instance, was not necessarily any lonelier than many a saint. There are also some who manage to reply to great questions for a time at least by making gods of their own bodies and prayer out of their pleasure. There are some very cheerful mystics, and there have always been a few who find an alien culture that seems to

68

offer them spiritual values which, like *vin de pays*, are not easy to export. As a matter of fact, surcease of loneliness comes to so many of us with a spiritual involvement (or an involvement that becomes spiritual) other than the orthodox ones that it sometimes seems to me we really are a polytheistic mob.

The feminist movement has given meaning to my life.

When you're 'in the tube' [the lip of a wave] of a big one, that's on a good day with good surf, I can't explain to you...it feels like...God...it feels like a beautiful lady, you know? It feels like nothing will ever feel better.

Since becoming a vegetarian, my whole life has opened up. It's more than just a physical thing.

These are quotations from interviews I've conducted this year for articles in various magazines. Not one of these interviewees, by the way, thought much about God (I always ask), beyond 'believing in "something"'; yet each of them had found what is apparently spiritual satisfaction, as well as fellowship, in something quite different.

It could be said, I guess, that it is unworthy to replace God's glory with nut cutlets, or a political movement, or even a towering Pacific wave — and maybe it is — but it also seems that a lot of those who worship God's glory are unclear about His spiritual function in the modern world. As an example of what I mean — not as proof, for there can't be any — I'll tell you that recently I found myself in central London one rainy afternoon, just as the pubs were closing. With me was a Born-Again, fervently Catholic friend whose home is near mine, and we were both in a desperate hurry to find a taxi to share. On a rainy afternoon in central London taxis are seen a little more frequently than giraffes. Suddenly I realized that what I had taken to be my friend's angry muttering was in fact a prayer, and then I discovered that what I had thought was a prayer was actually a request. 'Please, dear Jesus,' she was saying, 'would you send me a taxi?' As this friend is not particularly naive and, indeed, consorts with bishops, it was I, the atheist, who was appalled at such waste of God's grace, to say nothing of His time. Is there really much difference between this prayer and the statement of another acquaintance, a particularly earth-bound man, who told me that since taking a course in something called 'Mind Control' he has never failed to find a parking place for his car in downtown Los Angeles, so he knows that 'Mind Control' is the answer to all needs?

These days prayer seems to have the resonance of a radio phone-in, and the moving spirit could be a kind of traffic warden. Although some of us may find this vision of self in such outsize proportion to all else a perversion of faith which courts eventual loneliness and disappointment (to say nothing of damnation), I suppose the pragmatic agony aunt in me must advise that if it works and makes you feel better, don't knock it. When I'm not an agony aunt, however, I'm not so sure. It is the lack of spirituality about so much modern religion — as exemplified by my friend in the rain, by America's drive-in churches and switched-on clergymen, by programmes that play hymns by 'popular request', by door-to-door salesmen of grace — that suggests we crave religion instead of faith: we want ritual and dogma, but we do not want to risk the great loneliness of investigating the eerie significance of our souls. The current worldwide wave of Born Againism and fundamentalism is as much an expression of loneliness as it is of faith...maybe more. In other words, fundamentalism seems to be a rush away from individual confusion and back to some half-remembered communal safety. After a while, the dogma and ritual of a shared belief — be it a shared belief in Allah, or trades unions, or Manchester United — become their own purpose. Submission to dogma, which fundamentalism demands, entails what V. S. Naipaul calls 'loss of personality'. Personality is, after all, partly our own creation, developed through a multitude of choices that each of us is making all the time. Fundamentalism reduces those choices, in some cases to absurdity. 'Tell me about the coughing and the five principles [of Islam]' Naipaul asked a fundamentalist Muslim. He received this reply:

If you are in a gathering and you are ashamed to cough and three days later you wake up with a pain in your side because you didn't cough, that is wrong. It is mandatory to cough; if not, coughing is going to damage your health. Coughing is encourageable if you cover your mouth and say, 'Grace be upon Allah.' It is not encourageable to cough without covering your mouth. But to cough in somebody's face...is forbidden. It is un-Islamic and sinful....When you are by yourself and it doesn't offend anybody...you can stand up and cough or sit down and cough. It becomes entirely discretionary. All these things are regulated.[1]

Men and women joined in strict obedience to rules suffer 'loss of personality', and if they are bound by doctrine and discipline with no high spiritual purpose but only a political one (not to rescue but to convert, not to comprehend but to outlaw), how long before the community becomes authoritarian, even totalitarian? How long before those damaged in personality must elect a master or a god from among themselves?

I swear to thee Adolf Hitler...
Loyalty and bravery.
I vow to thee and to the superiors
Whom thou shalt appoint
Obedience unto death....[2]

So went the oath taken by a candidate who had passed into the SS. Provided with ritual, insignia, a sort of priesthood and a purpose, and relieved of all worrying questions by the discipline of obedience, SS men were not lonely. And any man who found himself thinking that in conscience he could no longer share the faith of his brotherhood was immediately in possession of a dissident and lonely secret that could, in short order, be the death of him.

In a relatively free society that has not stamped its image on every face and in every mind, the individual can think for himself, even if that should make him very lonely. In short, there is something infinitely worse than a godless society that fosters loneliness, and that is a god-fearing society that will not tolerate it.

10

The Silent Dialogue

> Thinking, existentially speaking, is a solitary
> but not a lonely business; solitude is that human
> situation in which I keep myself company.
> Loneliness comes about when I am alone with-
> out being able to split up into the two-in-one,
> without being able to keep myself company...
> or, to put it differently, when I am one and
> without company.
>
> Hannah Arendt, *The Life of the Mind*

Thinking is a dialogue a person has with his perpetual
companion: himself. It can consist of posing a proposition, sometimes in so many words or few words,
but more often in a shorthand of lightning speed,
and then replying to that proposition out of a body
of knowledge or the imagination. Sometimes thinking
takes place in writing; as a matter of fact, any writing
that isn't copying must always be thinking, for it
demands an original organization of concepts and
words that cannot be done with 'half a mind'. The
housewife shopping in the supermarket is thinking
too, and if she is in front of the frozen-food chest
judging two packets of, say, green beans for quality
and price, she is not at that moment lonely because

her mind, she would say if you disturbed her, is fully occupied.

Thinking is a solitary business, but it is painful and lonely only when the self is out of harmony with itself: when it is full of grief, or fear, or shame, and is alienated from itself, which makes it reluctant to be alone with itself. I know this all sounds recondite to the girl alone on Saturday night or the man who rings TIM just to hear a human voice; however, I am persuaded that if there is any lynchpin to loneliness, we are getting closer to it now.

When we cannot think, it is because we are, as we might say at those times, 'beside ourselves' or even 'out of our minds'. Anyone who has ever been in a frenzy of solitude and loneliness knows that it is, as Thoreau said, 'a slight insanity'. Hannah Arendt uses as an apt and glorious example of the troubled state that is desperate separation from self (loneliness) the following soliliquy from Shakespeare's *Richard III*:

What do I fear? Myself? There's none else by:
Richard loves Richard: that is, I am I.
Then fly: What! From myself? Great reason why:
Lest I revenge. What! Myself upon myself?

A man with thoughts as unharmonious and guilt-laden as these has got to be in a hurry to get away from himself: that is, to give the perpetual companion of his solitude the slip and to make himself unified and singular, which he can be only when in the company of other people.

Identity is not self. Identity is given us by others; self is our own. It isn't an inaccessible paradox to say we are least alone when we are with ourselves, when we split into the 'two-in-one' — when we are not that single entity others make of us — and that means the pain we call loneliness may come to us not because we lack the company of others but because we are pained by our own company and need to escape it. 'This original duality,' Hannah Arendt writes, 'explains the futility of the fashionable search for identity. Our modern identity crisis could be resolved only by never being alone and never trying to think.'[1]

A unified identity is something we can never really establish between us and ourselves because we are always changing, losing, gaining, and the illusion of an identity depends upon the way others see us. However, even that identity doesn't hold still, because each of us has numerous roles to play, and there will be numerous judgements passed on the way we play them. That a lot of these roles are played passively (nobody, for example, participates actively in being rhesus negative or having his name fall between 'k' and 'm' alphabetically; but being identified in this way can be of serious importance, though it affords no fellowship within the classification) doesn't make our search for identity any less confusing. Think of it! A man these days can be a good worker, a bad sport, an AB blood type, a Pisces, a learner driver, a steady drinker, a strong backhand, a Conservative voter, and knowing all that, who is he? Only very celebrated people looked upon with great respect have a more or less single and continuous identity in the eyes of virtually everyone. The Queen of England, for example, is a figure frozen by our awe into a consistently regal attitude, and anyone who happens to have intimate knowledge of her in any other attitude is sworn to secrecy.

It is fair to assume that the greater the discrepancy

between a public figure and his own private self, the more shame and fear awaits him in solitude: the more lonely he is. Thus the great general who must fire his troops with confidence in order to win battles finds all his own terrors waiting for him when he lifts off his helmet and sits alone but for the presence of himself or — since self debates all major issues with itself — the presence of his conscience. Thus too the loneliness of married homosexuals, say: is it the need for extramarital male company that makes them declare their loneliness or the need to be at peace in their own company? I honestly think it is the latter. There are men admired for public virtues who have private vices and whose solitude is therefore tormented by the battle of self with itself or by what we call a 'guilty conscience'. There are lots and lots of secret vices, but the ability to be comfortably alone without loneliness — that is, the ability to think — may be the only secret virtue.

It has got to follow then that society, the Church and the judgements of parents can actually create loneliness. The grown man who was persuaded as a child that he had to be perfect to be loved has got to hate being alone with his imperfect self, and, finding no harmony in the dialogue with his shameful other, he is destined to hate solitude, destined to be lonely unless he reconciles the two selves. Most of the 'crimes' that make solitude unbearable and create the frenzy of loneliness are infinitely less terrible than the sufferer imagines them to be, and many of them — such as homosexuality, for example, or hatred of a parent, or fear of failure, or disgust at some physical characteristic, or a million other dark secrets — are not crimes at all but only a general misunderstanding and intolerance of human behaviour (intolerance, by

76

the way, from which the suffering self is not immune and due to which it can hold itself in contempt). Tolerance and compassion would go much further to ease loneliness in the individual and in our society than any number of clubs, marriage bureaux or church socials. After all, what our society declares intolerable (sometimes with the greatest hypocrisy) the individual will not be able to tolerate in himself. In Albert Camus' novel *The Outsider* the protagonist, who is awaiting execution to which he has been sentenced, basically, for failing to weep at his mother's funeral, expresses essential loneliness. 'For all to be accomplished,' he says, 'for me to feel less lonely, all that remained was to hope that on the day of my execution there should be a huge crowd of spectators and that they should greet me with howls of execration.!

How often is shyness really the fear that one's 'terrible secret' or imagined inadequacy will be revealed to others? Most of the letters complaining of shyness that arrive on my desk seem to describe symptoms of shame: 'How can I stop blushing whenever I meet someone?' 'I freeze when I have to talk to people.' 'I'm too frightened to go to Weight Watchers' meetings.' The line between public shyness and private shame is so vague and wavering I am not sure it is always there at all; in fact, I could be convinced that shyness is often not simply fearing others but fearing oneself and fearing that the reasons one fears oneself — or the reasons one detests solitude, which is the company of oneself — will be apparent to other people. I used to be puzzled by the number of letters I received from teenagers complaining of acute shyness until I read R. D. Laing's chapter on self-consciousness in *The Divided Self*. 'The heightening or intensifying of the awareness of one's own being,' Laing writes, 'both as an object of one's own awareness and of the awareness of others, is practically universal in adolescents, and is associated with the well-known accompaniments of shyness, blushing, and general embarrassment.'[2]

Why shouldn't it be that adults who are still possessed of an adolescent's overblown awareness of self continue to suffer the same symptoms? Maybe the shy person ought not to imagine he lacks confidence but rather that he has an aggrandized notion of the attention he is receiving from others and, possibly, a guilty suspicion it is more attention than anyone actually deserves? I have always noticed that rather than hide away in private, some adults who continue to feel the swollen self-importance of adolescence learn to bluster, or bully, or perhaps even perform on a stage not so much to overcome their shyness — as they often maintain in interviews — as to indulge its gigantic self-consciousness. There is a popular theory that shyness is a form of arrogance; be that as it may, it seems clear to me that the arrogant adult is controlled by a shy adolescent within, who is still hopeful he is the centre of much more attention than is actually the case. Wouldn't it be a fine thing if we could say to the shy (and the arrogant) 'Grow up!', and if they immediately complied? But, of course, people who can grow up do grow up as much as they can. The best advice I would dare give anyone who suffers from shyness (or arrogance) would be that he must analyse it and think about it: it is thinking, after all, that makes us grow up.

Blushing, stammering, shaking in society, compulsive tics are all part of the dithering of an internal dialogue that is not harmonious. When lonely dithering goes haywire, sometimes even with dire brilliance, it is taken as evidence of breakdown and madness. Of all the human conditions I can imagine madness must be the most profoundly lonely, not because the madman has lost touch with others, but because he is divided from himself by a gulf of pain and terror. Even dying — an act that must be undertaken alone, that it is awful to contemplate and that separates us from all living creatures while uniting us with all nature — doesn't seem as lonely to me as the loss in life of self.

Philosophers do not slip leaflets through our letter-boxes. In what Hannah Arendt refers to as our 'fashionable search for identity' we are much less inclined to apply philosophy and poetry, which would reveal the hopelessness of our attempt, than we are to consult gurus and therapists, who profit from our attempt. As might be expected in acquisitive people who are detached from nature, we have more confidence in the magic we pay for than in the magic that is free, and so we pay for mantras, for spells, for systems that will help us 'find ourselves' as if we actually had to do anything more (or less) than look, feel and think for ourselves. But we no longer want general truths; each of us wants something specific to make *him* feel better and to present *him* with a gift-wrapped entity called 'identity'. We might as well be designing T-shirts with our own permanent mottos on them. The search for individual identity isn't much more than the search for an epitaph.

Self-identity is impossible to hold, for our only valid identity is the dual one — we and ourselves — and that must depend upon the changing, shifting, growing process of the internal dialogue called thinking. We are in a state of constant metamorphosis spiritually and intellectually, just as we are physically. Looking for self-identity is not only a futile pastime; in its ruthless selfishness it is even a pastime of dubious morality.

Conscience has fallen into disrepute (except among those afflicted by religiosity, who use the word dogmatically), but there is nothing else to call the register of inner harmony between 'us' and 'ourselves'. If we do not think — that is, if we avoid the dialogue with ourselves — then we are deprived of conscience, which is consciousness or personal awareness commonly of our effect upon others but also, and essentially, I think, of our effect upon ourselves. (In French, by the by, 'consciousness' and 'conscience' are the same word.) In the days before loneliness was our universal complaint, it was conscience — albeit regulated by religion — that kept each man in harmony with himself and all men in harmony with society. The individual now engaged in a 'fashionable search for identity' (and, it must be said, in the search for a fashionable identity) is self-aggrandizing, egotistical and ruthlessly ready to reverse the order established by wisdom and humility. In other words, it is his expectation that society should bestow on him a personal identity and what he imagines would then be an end to his loneliness. He never thinks that even if society could make him 'happy' and heal the schism between him and himself, why the hell should it?

When reading journals kept by people in the throes of a systematic search for identity — people, it's fair to say, who are avoiding at all costs that solitude in which they might be forced to think — I have been struck over and over again by two characteristics: first, philistinism, and then, cruelty. A few examples from statements made by people seeking their identity in Arthur Janov's once fashionable Primal Scream Therapy (since self-identity has become fashionable, fashions in methods of achieving it have become the hemlines of our psyches, moving up and down with bewildering speed!) ought to make the point that individual self-realization can be a most antisocial pursuit, adding to society's loneliness as well as to the list of trivial ways in which an individual can avoid thought and conscience.

One patient described her Primal Therapy in the following way: 'My whole life has been out of focus. Primals gave me the lens so that I could bring it all into focus. Everything is sharp and clear now. I'm smelling smells I never knew existed. For the first time my husband's BO is noticeable and bothersome.'

A patient who used to like opera became a rock-and-roll fan after his Primals [reports Janov with pride] 'More gutsy, more of the body,' he said. 'Now that I am alive I can't go with those operatic agonies any more.'[3]

It isn't just ineffectual deodorants and tenors that are at the source of alienation and neurosis, according to Janov's results. He quotes one of his enlightened patients as saying:

It occurred to me that the philosophers, the existentialists, and all the others didn't know what they were talking about when they tried to describe aloneness. There's no need for all these

81

multisyllabic terms they use. They are, in the final analysis, full of shit. So I started working with this feeling. My eyes were closed, and then something really great happened. I saw myself as a little boy of five or six or so, standing next to mother's bureau, looking up at her while she stood in front of the bureau's mirror in a bra, stuffed with her boobs, and adjusting the strings of her corset.[4]

If *that* is the 'final analysis', I hope I never get there. This 'really great happening' and insight into aloneness is devoid of the least general interest or application; it is tasteless and trivial, and even if it made the analysand and his analyst feel good for a moment, it did not apparently help his marriage much or ease the alienation his wife Susan must have been feeling (which, to use a favourite term of American analysands, was *her* problem.)

Susan wasn't talking to me and I didn't mind. More and more, I can see her sickness. What particularly is disturbing to me is her selfishness in bothering me when she should know how desperately important this whole Primal thing is.[5]

Let all charity and courtesy, conscience, wit and easing of the communal loneliness pass when an individual is searching for his identity!

All this agonizing and agony simply to avoid thinking! And all this pain simply not to recognize that the individual cannot perfect himself within an imperfect society, for he is part of his society and his society is part of him. The dialogue with self must be undertaken by each of us who wishes to avoid the pain of loneliness; conscience is freed by that dialogue, and the function of conscience must be to help us all create a more tolerant society. The unthinking man, hoping for an impossible wholeness and a permanent oneness, and believing this undertaking to be 'desperately important', is convinced he is at the centre of the universe, and the centre of the universe, even should it be ringing with Primal Screams, or EST insults, or a guru's chant, is one very lonely place to be. Especially since the universe has never paid the least attention to any one of us at all. There is a lot less loneliness and more fellowship in humility than in hubris.

It is out of date these days to talk about 'world views', yet this has got to be the view of the person who thinks, which is to say the conscious person, which is to say the person of true conscience — or, in other words, the person who can keep himself company. As the 'world view' always deals with essentials, and they are by their nature general, it is the only view that puts the thinking man in his place. And where is that but as one among myriad (a far less lonely place to be than an infant at the centre of a disdainful universe)? The man who thinks may never be more intellectual, more prosperous or even more popular than the unthinking man, but he will certainly be less lonely.

Thinking, though solitary, is a truly social act, for we think not in aid of self-realization but in aid of understanding. From increased understanding must come increased tolerance, and tolerance breaks down prejudices that alienate groups and individuals in our society. Most important, however, tolerance destroys barriers between 'us' and 'ourselves'. Nobody can sit around all day thinking; nevertheless, the great philosophical questions are not merely esoteric fol-de-rol; they come out of great human needs, and they can be applied to our individual needs. They are the issues — death, time, purpose, life — that swarm around people at four in the morning and drive the sleepless lonely then to telephone strangers and beg for help. Thinking is not an elitist activity, and it does not demand education. There are professors who never think, and there are scientists who are afraid to go home from the laboratory to thinking and conscience. Thinking is non-productive (which is far from saying is useless), without politics, non-conformist, but it eases loneliness by introducing self to itself.

> Thinking accompanies life and is itself the de-materialized quintessence of being alive; and since life is a process, its quintessence can only lie in the actual thinking process and not in any solid results or specific thoughts. A life without thinking is quite possible; it then fails to develop its own essence — it is not merely meaningless; it is not fully alive.[6]

It must seem to many people that Hannah Arendt and others like her overstate the case for thinking — that is, for improving the dialogue between self and itself — just as it seems to many that missionaries overstate the case for faith and lovers the case for love; nevertheless, for those who can do it, thinking gives purpose to life and it is purpose, and purpose alone, that makes light of loneliness.

11

Ideals and Raw Deals

> Love me or leave me and let me be lonely,
> I need your love and I need it only.
> I'd rather be lonely
> Than happy with somebody new.
>
> 'Love Me or Leave Me'

Loved or left? The opposite of sentimental love is loneliness, but as sentimental love is merely an invention and a conceit, then the kind of loneliness it causes and celebrates must be a phantom loneliness, a psychosomatic loneliness that hurts as much as any other, although it has its roots in imagination. The exclusive and romantic love that inspired the blues and torch-songs of our century entered the culture and tradition of this society, if not its very bones, long ago. Just like the wheel, purple sentiment has been so thoroughly integrated with our everyday life that we hardly realize it hasn't been there as long as man, and we find it hard to imagine that there are cultivated societies that do perfectly well without True Romance, just as the great Incas did without the wheel. In other words, there have been societies that did not roll, and there are still societies that do not need to glorify or justify a roll in the hay.

It seems to me that we owe the glorification
romantic love (and its concomitant loneliness
directly to the Judaeo-Christian belief that wicke
ness is implicit in sexual coupling, especially
of wedlock but also between married partners. T
current Pope says a husband can have 'adultero
thoughts about his own wife, but that he ought
to; and His Holiness supports the antique not
that in Heaven we will continue to be of two se
but without desire. Presumably, sexual appe
are held not to be heavenly but at their best f
tional and at their worst diabolical. The pagan
did not have to worry about such distinctions o
but, of course, his gods enjoyed their own se
genders...quite a lot, as a matter of fact. F
romantic sentiment is the pink sugar icing we
over that wormy cake which men (and wome
it could surprise the Pope to know) are appa
find themselves longing to taste. This hun
corrupt sweets of the flesh, which is how h
been seen by most of the founding fathers
Churches (and by the mothers, even thou
have hungered throughout time just as pass
for babies as for the means of getting the
ostensibly a result of the fall from grace. T
blues, and torch-songs, and lovesick sighs,
sobs of loneliness for a false lover, and pai
to an unfaithful mistress could be heard a
echoes of Adam and Eve's lament at fall
Paradise straight into each other's arms an
they'd made a bad deal.

Isn't it sad that because we so patently
inhibitions about sexual intercourse not
become mawkish in our attempt to glorify
but at the same time each sex blames an

the other for arousing shaming lust? 'He seldom errs', wrote the Scottish minister John Home, 'who thinks the worst he can of womankind,' and with this concise, though not dazzling, opinion men throughout literature and history would agree. On the other hand, Valerie Solanas writes in the Manifesto of the Society for Cutting Up Men:

Despising his highly inadequate self, overcome with intense anxiety and a deep, profound loneliness when by his empty self, desperate to attach himself to any female in dim hopes of completing himself, in the mystical belief that by touching gold he'll turn to gold, the male craves the continuous companionship of women. The company of the lowest female is preferable to his own.

If these two quotations represent extremes and seem to suggest that we are born from a conjunction of Neanderthal Man with Tokyo Rose, we mustn't forget that each sex has always had its own traditional lore that reveals a deep mistrust of the other.

'All men want just one thing,' (or a version thereof) have said how many mamas to their daughters?

'All cats are alike in the dark,' says papa to son.

'Isn't that just like a damn-fool woman?' say the men.

'My mama done tole me when I was in knee-pants that a man is a creature…a worrisome thing who'll leave you to sing the blues in the night,' trills the soprano.

'The girl that I marry will have to be as pink and as white as nursery,' replies the tenor.

Thus we all find ourselves looking for an end to loneliness in the very last place it might just conceivably be found: in the arms of an enemy. Not only do we gasp for lovers who have gone and call our longing loneliness, but many of us actually cry out for romantic love itself and call its absence loneliness. And if that One True and Only Love that is supposed to Last Forever turns out to be in fact only a shoddy substitute for something else, an illusion, a misinterpretation of a Roman joke, an umbrèlla over carnality that shames us all, it still doesn't prevent even the wittiest of us from thinking it sounds like fun. 'When love congeals,' wrote Cole Porter, a sophisiticated lyricist who saw (and saw through) the romantic urge, 'it soon reveals the faint aroma of performing seals/the double-crossing of a pair of heels/I wish I were in love again.' Mind you, only the gullible ever imagine they have actually found Perfect Love, and only the misguided marry for it.

Popular lyrics always seem to me to interpret what is happening in society's tin heart, and it is clear, even with pop's new interest in air pollution and Northern Ireland, that most of us are sentimentalists. Any life led without some spontaneous, irresistible lovemaking is inhibited possibly even to the point of neurosis; however, the fact remains that romantic love creates real, compulsive addicts. And since any amusement or painkiller can become a disease — frequently, in the case of the latter, the very one we took it to alleviate — romance addicts are frequently those among us who despise the opposite sex, or fear it, or do not actually find it desirable and need to excuse their loveless promiscuity as a search for a 'romantic ideal'. '…clinical experience shows beyond any doubt that those people who are incapable of establishing a lasting relationship are also dominated by an infantile fixation of their love relationships, in other words, suffer from a sexual disorder,' wrote Wilhelm Reich of the compulsory, promiscuous lover.[1] This disorder, he went on to say, can result from any of several neurotic compulsions, one of which is the obsessive pursuit of a 'phantasy ideal', and that means 'the disappointment which every sexual act brings anew prevents the establishment of a tender attachment to the partner.'[2]

The romantic addiction is unique in that the drug suffers as much as the addict, and maybe more. To be cast as the 'phantasy ideal' is to be passive and doomed. After all, the essence of an ideal is that it cannot ever be realized. The moment a perfect apple is tasted, it becomes flawed; the moment a perfect sunset is seen, it is changing; and the moment a perfect love is held in an embrace, it is debased by being possessed. So cruel romance claims its victims and is a purveyor of loneliness.

It is romantic love that depicts us as perpetual dancers waiting for that one enchanted evening when we will see at last, across the crowded room, that one stranger, the only one on earth who can turn loneliness into an eternal waltz. Yes, for the most part our romantic daydreams are just that banal.

His hand turned my face to meet his eyes. 'You needed someone last night, and I was there' [hundreds of thousands of breathless girls read in their copies of *True Romances* magazine in December 1981]. 'You need someone now, and I'm still here. Carol, please take what I offer...I need you in a way I can't explain....'

'I didn't plan last night, Tony. I only...couldn't believe what was happening to me. You make me

89

feel as though I'm caught in a whirlwind —'

'You are — and so am I,' Tony murmured as he kissed me. 'Think you can stand being caught in one for the rest of your life?'

This is not the pornography of emission but the porn of omission, and it would be no more than risible except for the very last paragraph of this little morality tale called 'Such an Attractive Neighbour' and many others just like it published every week.

So right there [says our heroine] ...my whole future was decided, because neither Tony nor I was the type to be cautious....And as far as we were concerned, loving and needing each other so much equalled marriage.

And what did marriage equal for this eager bride? Marriage equalled what it always has in fairytales: 'happiness ever after', with no more solitude or shame. What pernicious stuff this is! And what a store of agony and loneliness it lays in for the future, when ideals inexorably become raw deals.

Yet even banality like *True Romances* would not be such a lonely tragedy for those who believe Romance is True or that Truth is Romantic, if only this trash were read and believed by both sexes. 'It hadn't been easy, sticking to the promise I'd made myself — to wait to make love until our wedding night,' the female readership breathes with the teenaged heroine of 'The Unhappiest Day of My Life!' in *Romance* magazine. 'So many times I'd wished that I'd never even thought of it. Yet, now that my wedding was coming nearer, I felt glad that we had waited. Maybe it was terribly old-fashioned.

But it was right for us.' Our heroine is the one, by the by, who thought of saving sex for the honeymoon, so it does seem a little presumptuous of her to assume that the sacrifice was 'right for *us*', and if she continues to make such central decisions without consulting her partner, the marriage doesn't stand a chance. What had her fiancé thought about such restraint, after all? Permit one of his own romantic magazines, *Penthouse*, to tell us of his expectations: 'the one man who'd won Connie's heart took long…looks before he leaped,' write the editors of their gatefold fantasy. 'When the lovemaking finally began, though, the fireworks went off in rapid — and multiple — succession (if we know what she means).'

I certainly don't envy *Romance* and *Penthouse* daydreamers the True Love they find together, and I suspect the future holds some very unpleasant surprises for both of them.

The ideals of romantic love are downright unfriendly in a society where there is already much reason to complain of each other's neglect. Romantic love demands that men and women should remain as different from each other as they can, even against personal inclination; and since every division in society adds to misunderstandings and the tinder of loneliness, romantic sentimentality actually increases real loneliness in two ways. First, it increases the differences and alienation between the sexes and, second, it widens the breach between an individual's inner and outer worlds — that is, between who he is with himself, and who he hopes he is seen as being by others. It is in these spaces between people, but even more between self and itself, that loneliness rages.

The romantic belief that on the whole of this planet each man is intended for the one specific woman who is intended for him sharply divides men from women. And what could more fatally intensify the wound of incompleteness within individuals that is the source of loneliness than a spurious healing of it, than the notion that two people of the opposite sex can and must meet to form a psychical and spiritual whole, as two sexual partners can briefly and roughly make a physical entity? If in a crowded world there really were but one he for each she, predestination would have to play a vital role in every meeting, and that is why romantic love is conducive to superstition and to an attitude of helplessness.

Entire advertising campaigns are based on the magical apparition of a man on a white horse as soon as a girl anoints herself with the right kind of bath oil or when she has a yen for soft-centred chocolates. Superstitious people are people who just cannot help themselves from committing the most cruel and barbarous mischief upon any who stands in the way of predestined True Love. For is True Love not the power that must never be gainsaid? And when two people are terribly, terribly in love, according to their kismet are they not the minority that rules and overrules? Now, a practical and experienced old agony aunt like me figures the last thing any of us needs these days is to believe in magic, to expect a miracle without expending faith or energy to bring it about. People who begin to believe they 'just cannot help themselves' are destined to be lonely on every level, failing even to avail themselves, when True Love falters or does not arrive on schedule, of clubs, marriage bureaux and

and other well meaning activities that might distract them from the threat of solitude and the fear of isolation.

In the discrepancy between the ideal lover and the real, complex, imperfect, fallible lover loneliness thrives. Instead of considering the source of our loneliness, which remains the space within, we are enticed by advertised fantasies to consider the space between us and the romantic ideal of another — a *Penthouse* 'pet' or a man on a white charger — who is himself a romantic ideal. Thus we are enticed to design ourselves according to what we think an impossibly wonderful other will cherish and — since our romantic fantasies are limited and not very original — according to a general stereotype of desirability. By trying to make ourselves desirable to a fantasy (a film star, maybe, or a sheikh, or the girl next door, or just Mr Right), we try to make of ourselves a fantasy; and in doing that we make it harder for the dialogue between us and ourselves to take place in good conscience, and thus we increase the space within where loneliness does swell. This is why the pseudo-playboy can sit surrounded by hi-fi speakers, alone, pining for his gatefold dream. And this is why agony aunts receive so many letters from young women in real distress after discovering girlie magazines among their boyfriends' possessions. Each one of those air-brushed, plastic cuties is a reminder of how the real girl, who is marked more by calories than a bikini, falls short of her beloved's ideal or fantasy. I am constantly surprised by the number of letters I receive from women who say that having found such a cache under the bed, they never again want their lovers to touch them. Their agony is twofold: first, they have lost the illusion that their man is the pure yet strong, gentle yet dominating, experienced yet uncorrupted lover of *Romance* magazine; and, second, they have no faith that they can be the object of his attention when his romantic fantasy is apparently such a superior product.

So it is that romantic rubbish piles up between us and ourselves and creates the lonely condition of shame where shame ought not to exist. Women become ashamed of bodies they fear will be found less desirable than those on page three and try to hide them. Men become ashamed of 'weaknesses' or sexual predilections they have been told are hardly romantic. And in an ultimate convulsion of paradox, the beloved who is ashamed not to be the ideal the other has taken him for becomes a little contemptuous of his lover for being deceived.

Now that tradition has freed us commoners at least to marry for romantic trivia instead of for gain, or to please our parents, or to extend an inheritance, our divorce rate soars. Why? It isn't marriage that is failing us but the fantasy of romantic love, that blinding light that dazzles lovers and fades before the very eyes of brides and grooms. If the liberation of women is actually contributing to the divorce rate, and many maintain that it is, it appears to me to be not because women want to be independent in order to find their own destinies, and not because women's liberation threatens men's enslavement of them, and not because strong women are too much for weakened men to pin down — as if men and women could not be strong at the same time (well, ought they not at least try to be?) — but because men and women are for the first time free to make marriages based on romantic fantasies rather than on class, common sense, ambition or the wishes of their parents. And if all this seems out of the way in a book about loneliness, we must remind ourselves that wherever there is a divorce, at least one person is very lonely.

12

Confronting Consciousness

> It is sometimes less difficult to wake up and feel that I am alone when I really am than to wake up with someone else and be lonely.
>
> Liv Ullmann, *Changing*

Loneliness is not simply the absence of others or another, and so it is not 'cured' by the presence of others or another. Adam and Eve, whatever else they may have been, are useful symbols in an apt and persuasive allegory of our condition. Outside Paradise they were not deposited at opposite ends of their globe from each other; they were made wretched, confused and lonely together. Moreover, the experience of the first generation born in exile does not suggest that family life then was necessarily bliss and solace any more than it is now.

We establish relationships in the hope of easing loneliness but, in fact, a lot of us go on maintaining painful or dull relationships solely because we are so terrified of being alone, and we lack the courage to use the wonderful line Arthur Miller gave Marilyn Monroe in *The Misfits*: 'If I'm gonna be alone, I'd rather be by myself!' We fear an increase of pain in the absence of another, even if the other is a boorish or uncongenial partner. The very fear of loneliness causes as much misery as loneliness itself, and maybe more: fear of loneliness *is* loneliness. Being alone, however, is not necessarily lonely.

Many people, when pressed, admit that what fear of loneliness without a partner really amounts to is the 'shame' of being seen alone in a society arranged for the comfort of couples and families. This shame, by the way, is as prevalent among men as it is among women, because a man seen often alone is considered (or considers himself to be considered) a sexual deviant; a woman on her own, if she is thought about at all, is simply pitied. After all, a person alone is theoretically living without sexual sport. For a man this is considered distinctly unnatural behaviour, while even in days like these, clamouring for sexual equality, a woman alone is merely thought pathetic, quaint or, if she is at all attractive, a 'waste'.

Whatever the emotions are — fear, desire, curiosity, lust, hope — that propel two people into each other's embrace and merge briefly their two struggling egos, they must pass. Emotions do pass. And when they have gone, we find it very hard to remember what the fuss was about, as anyone who keeps a diary and rereads it from time to time will know. When the emotions that established a relationship pass, a pair of confused and hostile strangers can find themselves meeting suddenly in bed or across the breakfast table, each sunk in misery, disappointment and loneliness. 'At last I see you for what you really are!' one may say to the other. But the truth is that each is being confronted by his own dead pretensions and the shed skin of his own ego. At this very point a lot of married couples decide to divorce, and since second marriages have a disaster rate just as high as first marriages, the suggestion is that few of them have learned to take responsibility for themselves, and most of them are still expecting another person to create that inner harmony which is the only end to loneliness and which, I have not a doubt in the world, each of us must make for himself. Mind you, since it is estimated that about 85 per cent of divorced men (considerably fewer women with children) will remarry, and often to someone they met during the marriage, it's hard to see just when in all this overlapping of relationships they will have an opportunity to encounter themselves in solitude and find out what they think about themselves.

I remember hearing a film actress, married for the fourth time, say to a viewing audience of millions: 'This time it's the real thing! In this relationship I've found myself at last!' How very puzzling that sounded to me! Hell, if it really was herself she had always been looking for, then she must have been looking in some very odd places, since, God knows, the rest of us had difficulty avoiding her. And if it was herself she thought she'd found at last in the person standing at her side, then she wasn't seeing very clearly, for he was ten years younger than she, considerably prettier, taller, and besides he was a man. Judging from an intoxicated fire in his eyes, the only thing he and she had in common was a massive self-importance.

'Relationship', in the sentimental sense, is a relatively new addition to the common language. Not long ago the only 'relationships' between the sexes were formed by birth or business. (Marriage was counted a business, and until this century sexual passion was expressed outside marriage, like as not, in another kind of business.) Of course, men and women have fallen madly in love with each other over the ages; the most fervent of these unions have been chilled in poetic amber, which is the only way I can think of in which passion outlasts time. Formerly, most fierce attractions between the sexes either became 'love affairs', a much more explicit term than 'relationships' (and in a sense, therefore, much less romantic), or they dwindled into sensible unions with parental blessings. Once in a while great lovers were star-crossed and pined away, or killed themselves, or grew indifferent and in due course found someone else. Only two decades ago, before 'relationships', teenagers were afflicted by a condition called 'puppy love' rather more often than they were by venereal disease.

Today everyone wants a 'relationship', and this choice of euphemism is interesting because it rings with a brainy resonance lacking in mere 'love affair' or even in commonplace marriage. 'Relationship' suggests equality between the partners and manages to hint at an absence of exclusivity that marks most mating. 'Relationship' is a fashionable, on-going, situational kind of word at this moment in time; it is hopeful of some better understanding between the sexes undertaking it, yet it sounds pretentious because it suggests that hope has been realized. In fact, the chief difference between a 'relationship' and an old-fashioned 'love affair' is that a 'relationship' is apparently less likely to end in marriage, and when it does, the marriage is more likely to end in divorce.

A 'love affair' used to be based honestly, if dangerously, on romantic or sexual excitement; a marriage used to be based on compatible ambitions. On what do we base a 'relationship'? Largely, it seems to me, on our troubling awareness of the empty room within. However, when two people who demand privacy (for 'relationship' suggests that each partner is going to have his 'space') but who have learned no tolerance or respect for solitude — two people, in other words, who have not developed qualities of independence — when these two enter a 'relationship' with each other, they are racing downhill. They cannot see each other. Each is looking for the other to identify him. They are like two opposing mirrors, reflecting and blind. The only way enduring friendship can ever transcend the unresolved fears and jealousies that lurk under a 'relationship' is for each partner to be able to see the other honestly, or at least for one of the partners to be capable of this honesty and to accept the burden of the other's fantasies. In an ideal relationship both partners know they can live perfectly well without each other, but they also know they much prefer to live with each other.

Being able to see ourselves and each other as complete people does not prevent loneliness even within our 'relationships', but it can allow us to acknowledge and contemplate the loneliness that must be there, and it spares us the frenzy of trying, trying, trying again to dispel the truth: the truth is that we are alone here. Love for each other sweetens our lives, but it does not change the essential nature of them.

The apartness of lovers and their separateness even within the most passionate involvement, the impossibility of melting one life and one consciousness with another, is something we must learn to respect, for it is indeed 'incurable'. If love between men and women is ever to have the majesty of great friendship, then men and women will have to see each other clearly, not seek in each other what they think they lack in themselves, and not find in each other a means of achievement or gratification.

In other words, the only justification we can have for our favourite new word 'relationship' is to relate consciously to someone other than ourselves, to see that person in the clear light of day, to be seen and to acknowledge our separateness. All else will be failure. With this recognition of innate separateness must come an end to waking up with someone else and feeling lonely because that person is a stranger. See the other, listen to the other, know the other, like him or love him; he may be a liar, but it cannot hurt us that he is a stranger. The very joy of separateness from the other is to be able to undertake the long, slow uniting of what has been separate; this is the undertaking we can justifiably call a 'relationship' unless we have the courage to call it love. However, first we must know we are separate and see the other as separate and unburdened with our fantasies. First we must realize, accept and even investigate our own separateness. First, we must achieve a degree of independence, and that means in part that we must not fear solitude or be ashamed of it but must accept it and our innate loneness as the conditions of our birth.

We cannot *have* each other or fill the empty room with each other. We cannot even know each other's thoughts. When we think we do, we are only projecting our own hopes or fears on to the other: we are still loving foolishly and dangerously. We can be enriched by each other's knowledge, experience, wit, company, charm, even by each other's money; but when the beloved bites an apple, the lover cannot taste it, and when he tastes the apple, he can be sure it is not as it tasted to his beloved. We can share space, ambitions, children, opinions, appetites, our last crumb or cigarette, but when a lover dreams, he dreams alone. We can appreciate each other in practical ways, in fanciful ways, in sex, in laughter, but when a lover suffers, his beloved may weep but cannot feel the pain. Love actually intensifies our separateness from others and from the other if only because it makes us long deeply and hopelessly to abolish the space between us and the other. It makes us crave the paradox, for if love is to endure, it can only be between two people who are conscious and even proud of their existential separateness. If not, if love is undertaken as a distraction from loneliness or a 'cure' for the very separateness it ought to celebrate, then love must disappoint, and the affair is only a nod between strangers.

If more marriages were seen as genuine relationships — that is to say, as matings of 'her' and 'me' or 'him' and 'me' rather than the film star's mating of 'me' with 'myself' — then fewer marriages would end in divorce. Divorce represents failure and, like all failure, it isolates people in their disappointment and humiliation: it makes them feel the pain of their separateness where they never felt its benefits. Only artists have been granted the gift of distracting themselves from the lonely pain of failed love by making something of it. Most of us have to give the wound time to heal and try to use that time not to find a replacement for the lost lover but to find ourselves. How do we find ourselves? By looking very hard and probably all alone. By experimenting in order to find out what it pleases us to do, what it interests us to learn and what it will interest and please us to share.

To move towards relationships in which lovers see each other and recognize their apartness obviously means we must finally abandon our pursuit of those romantic stereotypes which have for a long time encouraged dishonesty. This doesn't mean that men must become more 'feminine' and women more 'masculine', but only that we should let the trashy, romantic significance of these adjectives drift away so each of us is free to become more who he is becoming and less who he thinks he is expected to be.

13

Settlers in No-Man's-Land

I have seldom, very seldom, crossed this border-land between loneliness and fellowship. I have even been settled there longer than in loneliness itself. What a fine bustling place was Robinson Crusoe's island in comparison!

Franz Kafka, *Diary*, 25 October 1921

Virtually every loss makes us isolated and lonely: loss of nature, loss of God, loss of each other and loss of self. Of course, there are special conditions of loss, such as loss of health, bereavement, loss of mobility or one of our senses, that bring crises of isolation and loneliness. Finally, there is the loss that all aware people share: time's passing and carrying us away with it, particle by particle. The old-age pensioner, for whom we are urged to spare a thought at Christmas, is lonely for company, yes, but the loss of his energy, his ambition, his influence and his vitality is very nearly complete, and he misses them. To some extent each of us is lonely for the person he was yesterday, and to this extent we are all lonely. To some extent each of us is missing the person he imagined himself to be yesterday or the person he dreamed he would be, and at least to this extent we are all lonely.

I do not intend to minimize aspects of our society that encourage loneliness. Certainly, to a degree those conditions are under our control, and if we cannot effect legislation against loneliness, we can do our best to support humane and tolerant reforms of the institutions that often thrust into solitude and agonized isolation those least equipped to cope. There is every reason why those of us who are a little less inhibited should reach out to the more inhibited — and I do mean everything from volunteer hospital visiting to talking to each other in bus queues. However, I consider pity a base emotion, and so I think those who want to 'do good' for others must constantly review their motives. In my own observation, doing good, if it is not done brilliantly with genuine altruism, creates righteousness and power on one side, subservience and justifiable resentment on the other.

Nor am I absolutely sure that doing something about repressive aspects of society will necessarily make people less lonely. For example, the walls between classes continue to tumble, and those still standing, such as private education, are under attack; maybe in the long run tolerance and brotherhood will grow out of the rubble. For what it's worth, I doubt it. But I'm getting older and crotchety. Born on the threshold of the Second World War, I've seen no evidence whatsoever that tolerance or brotherhood are ever to be found in polity or institutions; only (and rarely) are they found in the individual. Could we be turning increasingly to our governments to provide qualities that we, as individuals, don't bother to nurture in ourselves? Racial and sexual tolerance, for instance, freedom of speech and religion, peace, fellowship and even happiness are more likely to turn up as campaign promises than as personal aims. Marriage counselling is available on the National Health because couples don't seem to care to work very hard at living together, and the suburban air is thick with sponges being thrown in.

Creating a new class, such as the class of children, always creates a new area of isolation, as I've said; however, it would be glib and doctrinaire to assume that doing away with that class or any other would in a practical way correct loneliness. Class, whatever its inquities, is cosy. Within the class structure there has been fellowship — from working men's clubs to the Athenaeum — and one of the reasons why so many people now complain of the kind of loneliness that comes from lack of fellows is precisely that the class systems have to a great extent broken down. After all, who are a man's fellows? Once upon a time, and not very long ago, it was easy for him to know: his fellows were men of his own background in education, in work, financially and politically. He recognized them cheerfully, whatever his bitterness about the other classes. A class was hedged off and private. But now? The idealists say that all men will discover their common fellowship in an egalitarian welter, and that is a moving and beautiful concept; however, the average man speaks the language of only a tiny percentage of all men, trusts a vastly smaller percentage, counts himself as the most important of all men and doesn't consider women or children men at all.

Just now most of us are out of our class and floundering around in the great, unstructured middle. We are no longer born into villages, big families, small specialist communities with ready-made companions, or even strictly delineated social classes. This freedom to move is a fine thing for the strong but no better than ever, maybe even worse, for the weak. We are born into a threatening crowded jungle, where we must instruct our children never to talk to strangers or to take their sweets. But if we do not ever talk to strangers, and if we tend more and more to live in private units of one, or a couple, or a few, protected by police and government and social services, then to whom can we talk? Who will be our fellows?

BY ALL MEANS DO TALK TO STRANGERS! It is a self-indulgence to write that suggestion because it is one of the few pieces of advice I often long to give those who write to me calling themselves lonely. But I do not dare to do it because too much loneliness is bound up parasitically with self-pity, and some loneliness is honestly attached to real and dangerous inadequacies. Those who need loneliness to prove their ineptitude or their anger — 'Poor me. Nobody loves me. People are rotten. You see how they neglect poor me?' — are precisely the ones who might go out on my advice and talk to the wrong strangers. It is this sort of bindweed loneliness that often comes to the attention of agony aunts and other popular advisers. When loneliness is the emotion a man chooses to feel in order to prove to some unknown power, or to himself, that he is being hard done by, then he has a great investment in continuing to be lonely, and there is every chance the strangers who respond to him will either be condescending or con-men.

Among the habits of independence recommended hopefully are two key qualities: intuition and spontaneity. Anyone who has developed these qualities doesn't need me to explain that talking to strangers is precisely where fellowship lies. Where else but from among strangers can we find friends? The clear current of intuition receives a stranger without reference to pretensions, which is to say not that the intuitive person is without pretensions but only that he has the knack of suspending them. Californians used to call intuition getting another's 'vibrations', and that seems to me a fine description of the process. So very like love is friendship that I continue to be surprised it is so rare between the sexes and can only assume we cannot like what we desire, or see clearly when we desire. Maybe when we are desiring we are too interested in ourselves.

If women have in the past at least possessed a greater degree of intuition than men, that is probably because whatever our feminine vanities, life has not encouraged us to be blinded by self-importance. How self-important is a person likely to be who is not conventionally destined to keep the surname she was born with? And, since part of intuition's duty is to keep us a step ahead of danger, to some extent we women have developed intuition to accompany us on lone journeys and down dark city streets.

Incidentally, Dr John Nicholson, a psychologist, delivered a paper all about friendship to the 1981 British Psychological Society Conference, in which he discussed some differences in the ways men and women make their friends. Women, it seems, make close friends early on through relatives and existing friends (where *they* come from, he didn't specify), while men make their friends at school, at university and at work. I can't say I was amazed by this trend, but I assume that as more women go to university and go to work, more women will make friends there. The doctor also discovered that men, as they age, tend to shed their work friends and turn to the neighbours, which, if we think about it, could signify a turning in maturity from competition to comfort. Nevertheless, the most friendless people in our society, according to this survey of 550 inhabitants of Colchester,[1] are men in their forties, nearly half of whom said they were totally friendless. Only a third of the women interviewed were without friends. I suspect this is partly because we women are intuitive, and also because we see ourselves as a class, within which there is sisterhood. Who knows? Maybe when we are finally liberated out of our class into 'equality', we will be just as friendless as men.

Spontaneity is the spirit to act on intuition. Intuitive and spontaneous people cannot be lonely in the ordinary sense because making friends, or even just accumulating acquaintances, is an intuitive and spontaneous process. How a person learns to be intuitive and spontaneous is not something an agony aunt can explain. I could give detailed advice on cooking meals for those who live alone (I'll bet a lot of you wish I would!), or how to structure a lonely day, or the kinds of hobbies lonely people can pursue, even on the kind of thoughts lonely people can think, but I cannot tell anyone specifically how to go about making friends, so I'll continue to speak generally.

Generally, it is necessary honestly to want friends before we find them, and that means to be ready for a commitment of self and energy. Kafka wrote in his diary on one occasion:

I sat apart, a perfect stranger....I could have availed myself of invitations to take part in society, even, to an extent, public life; everything required of me I should have done, if not well, at least in

109

middling fashion...yet I refused. Judging by this, I am wrong when I complain I have never been caught up in the current of life....I should probably have refused every offer.[2]

Kafka had his purpose in not seeking fellowship, which can in some circumstances be an unwelcome distraction. To find friends, a man must first make of himself a potential friend. Making oneself a friend demands a degree of sacrifice and self-effacement that some people would rather not allow. Kafka was a moody son-of-a-bitch and, judging from his diaries, his moods were necessary to his art. It is very hard to imagine him the contented bridge player, the selfless lover and the good chum, as well as the author of *The Trial*. A lot of us have less than art at stake, and yet we have reasons of our own not to donate what fellowship requires: energy, time, interest and self. For one thing, we may be terrified of rejection. To offer self and have that offer turned down is a stinging humiliation; and afterwards to offer self again, and perhaps again, demands extra courage. Only the man in a corner of the room who makes conversation with nobody can be sure nobody will reject him. When that man then complains to people like me in the most aggrieved tones that, yes, he does go out but nobody ever talks to him, I can only tell him to talk first. However, between telling him to talk and telling him what to say (for that will be his next question) is a narrow space that contains for me the difference between interest and arrogance.

I cannot recommend topics for conversation with strangers the way I might a particular after-shave. Making ourselves interesting is something each of us has to do all by himself. Isn't it an odd kettle of fish that for any personable man or woman, a smaller investment of self or imagination is required to attract a new lover than to attract a new friend? I remember once spending an entire evening being enchanted by a visiting Berliner before it dawned on me, with my forty words of German, that his English was practically non-existent.

We become interesting through our interests. Unfortunately, it is not necessarily attractive to be interested merely in having friends, for that is but an extension of self-interest, but it is attractive to have an interest that congenial people will share. What good is joining the local dramatic society, for instance, without a genuine interest in theatre? Anyone who applies himself to *The Mousetrap* solely in the hope of finding friends is going to be disappointed and disappointing. Making of oneself a friend for friends to discover entails making of oneself a person with something to share other than loneliness. It seems self-evident, yet innumerable letters come my way from people complaining they have joined everything from swimming clubs to the Church of England and still they are friendless, and what do I have to say about *that*?

How do we find our interests? In conference with ourselves. And those who are interested in nothing at all — in no sport, no art, no work, no other people, no amusements, no politics — must be terribly interested in their own misery and had better just resign themselves to being in their own company.

Many years ago an American named Dale Carnegie wrote a book that has since been a perennial best-seller called *How to Win Friends and Influence People*. I have never read this book and I can't imagine I ever shall. I don't find the title promising. However, millions of people found it irresistible. The very

111

idea the qualities that attract friends, who seem to me to be as close as any individual comes to being an equal, are the same qualities that bring admiration, power and, practically by definition, envy, I find alien and worrying. (Mind you, could it, I wonder, account for the 48 per cent of Dr Nicholson's aggressive, competitive mid-life males who claim they are friendless?) Honest friendship is based on a willingness to give as well as to receive, and if that sounds straight from the pen of Pollyanna, I must add that willingness to do something doesn't always accomplish it. Willingness is like hope: we can fail with it, but without it we haven't a chance. The willingness to give time, effort, affection and attention to another person is probably not as common among us as it could be in a less acquisitive and ambitious society where giving might actually be considered as rewarding as giving-and-taking. Friendship, for instance, can demand not only that we make the first move but also that we are prepared to make some extra ones.

We are as often afraid of being cheated and getting less than we think we should get as we are afraid of being humiliated by a rejection. The fear of being 'done' or taken advantage of destroys spontaneity and prevents us from trusting our intuition. Thus when I receive letters from people complaining that their offers of friendship are not being snapped up on the open market, I feel compelled to remind them that they appear not to be giving of themselves but only offering themselves in trade. Spontaneity is not reckless, and intuition is first cousin to common sense. We need to use caution in our dealings with strangers (this is no society of angels), but we do not need suspicion until the stranger has offered us good reason for it.

112

14

Conclusion

> I'll get one of those bachelor-type apartments, and I'll fix it all up! I'll get a bullfight poster, and I'll get some of that black furniture. Did ya ever see that real sharp black furniture? Real nice, you know? And I'll…get a pearl-white phone…and I'll just sit back and relax, and finally, I'll be all alone! All alone…
>
> Lenny Bruce

Maybe we will all find what we are missing, and maybe any one of us will regain what he has lost, but from here it's hard to see those things happening. The image of a stern, protective God, for example, appears to be passing now except in a few medieval bastions and among clutches of intellectuals. If a new version of a deity is being created, it's not likely to emerge from the fashion for fundamentalism, which is by definition reactionary, or out of the dogma of pseudo-religions such as Scientology, or from the pronouncements of senile gurus. And if any of these should be where the replacement for the old faiths will come from, then God help us, for we will be adrift with a paper anchor.

As for nature, it seems our home improvements

alienated us from her, even though she awaits us with patience and regards in silence the non-biodegradable ruins we are making. Nature doesn't miss us, being able to get along very well without us, but we do miss her and we miss being gainfully employed in her dominion, since so much of what we must do now seems 'unnatural', mechanical and even explosively anti-nature.

So we are lonely for God and lonely for nature. Moreover, we have less and less to share with our children except a general impression that all is not well. In fact, many parents are so puzzled by their children that they have begun to feel it is they themselves, rather than the younger generation, who are the innocent newcomers. Not just the generations but the sexes too grapple with each other, though not in order to discover love and fellowship; on the contrary, more often than not it is to act out lonely fantasies and then blame each other for their failure.

We are lonely for each other. We want privacy, but we dread solitude. We are in pursuit of an 'identity', and we use a lot of energy excavating for it, as if it were a treasure and not just fairy gold; on the other hand, we think conscience, contentment and independence — qualities we ought in fact to be forging for ourselves — should be given to us free.

Is life all unrelieved gloom? Only if we succumb to the modern notion that it *ought* to be happy and that happiness is a right rather than an achievement (even the American Constitution, a most idealistic document, speaks of a man's right to the '*pursuit* of happiness', which is a far cry from happiness itself); or if we allow ourselves to imagine that friendship is a department of the social services rather than a personal donation each of us makes; or if we choose

114

to believe that loneliness is a disease that must have a cure rather than a condition of existence and knowledge. I suppose by now it is clear that I think true loneliness has very little to do with lack of fellows and almost everything to do with an inability to be alone. Lack of fellows may be an itch, but failure to be content in one's own company is a flaming agony. All the clubs, the parties, the friends, the pussy cats and aspidistras, all the agony aunts cannot make anyone one whit less lonely if he is unwilling or unable to hunt for joy and revelation where they are hiding: within himself.

Why all this panic, dread and horror of being alone? When you are alone, what is there to fear? When you are alone, you are all by yourself. Honestly, what can threaten you when you are alone?

Notes

1 Utopians in Exile

1 Shiva Naipaul, *Black and White* (London: Hamish Hamilton, 1980), p. 207.
2 Frederick S. Perls, *Gestalt Therapy Verbatim* (New York: Bantam Books, 1971), p. 4.

2 All the Lonely People

1 Ira A. Tanner, *Loneliness: the Fear of Love* (New York: Harper & Row, 1973), p. 75.
2 Tony Lake, *Loneliness* (London: Sheldon Press, 1980), p. 30.

3 Childhood: a New Estate

1 Ivan Illich, *Deschooling Society* (London: Calder & Boyars, 1971), p. 26.
2 Carl Jung, *Memories, Dreams, Reflections* (London: Fontana, 1972), p. 58.
3 ibid., pp. 219-20.

4 Heirs to Loneliness

1 A. S. Neill, *Summerhill — a Radical Approach to Education* (Harmondsworth: Penguin, 1970).

5 Solitude: Privation or Privilege?

1 Bruno Bettelheim, *Children of the Dream* (St Albans: Granada, 1971).

6 Missions of Discovery

1 David Reuben, *Everything You Always Wanted to Know about Sex* (New York: Bantam, 1971), p. 218.
2 Paul Theroux, *The Old Patagonian Express* (Boston: Houghton Mifflin, 1979), p. 391.

7 Accursed Activity

1 Michael Korda, *Charmed Lives* (London: Allen Lane, 1980), p. 355.
2 Henri Troyat, *Tolstoy*, trs. N. Amphoux (Harmondsworth: Penguin, 1970), p. 415.

8 A Slight Insanity

1 Lynn Shahan, *Living Alone and Liking It* (New York: Stratford Press, 1981).

9 Faith or Fellowship?

1 V. S. Naipaul, *Among the Believers: an Islamic Journey* (London: André Deutsch, 1981), p. 158.
2 Heinz Hohne, *The Order of the Death's Head* (London: Pan, 1972), p. 135.

10 The Silent Dialogue

1 Hannah Arendt, *The Life of the Mind* (London: Secker & Warburg, 1978), p. 185.

2 R. D. Laing, *The Divided Self* (Harmondsworth: Penguin, 1965), p. 106.
3 Arthur Janov, *The Primal Scream* (London: Sphere Books Ltd., 1974), pp. 156, 157.
4 ibid., p. 180.
5 ibid., p. 181.
6 Hannah Arendt, *The Life of the Mind*, p. 191.

11 Ideals and Raw Deals

1 Wilhelm Reich, *The Sexual Revolution* (New York: Noonday Press, 1967), p. 120.
2 ibid.

13 Settlers in No-Man's-Land

1 *Guardian*, 23 December 1981.
2 Martin Greenberg (trs.), Max Brod (ed.), *Franz Kafka* (London: Secker & Warburg/Octopus, 1976), p. 847.

X